◆ THE VEGETARIAN FEAST ◆

ELAINE BASTABLE

◆C·O·N·T·E·N·T·S◆

First published in 1985 by Octopus Books Ltd
59 Grosvenor Street, London W1
Fourth impression 1986

© 1985 Hennerwood Publications Ltd
ISBN 086273 198 4
Printed in Hong Kong

◆I·N·T·R·O·D·U·C·T·I·O·N◆

Interest in the cooking and eating of meals without meat is growing steadily, as many of us come to the conclusion that a healthy diet does not necessarily need to include meat, poultry or fish. As a result, vegetarianism's slightly eccentric image has faded in recent years and many more people are interested in vegetarian recipes. But first what is a vegetarian? It is someone who does not eat the flesh of animals or any products resulting from the killing of animals, which includes ingredients such as suet, lard or gelatine. Vegetarians (or lacto-vegetarians to be absolutely accurate) do include a moderate amount of dairy foods in their diet and, of course, eggs. A far stricter group are known as vegans. They eat only natural foods such as beans, grains, nuts, vegetables and fruit – no animal products, including dairy foods, of any kind. Reasons for choosing to become vegetarian vary enormously. For many, the thought of breeding and killing animals simply for food is abhorrent. Others are disturbed by the conditions in which the animals are bred and feel that the food produced by such methods causes unnecessary suffering to the animals concerned. Others feel that the agricultural resources of the world could best be used to grow grain for human consumption rather than to feed animals for slaughter; less meat for the Western world could mean sufficient grain to feed the Third World. There is also, of course, a large number of people who just do not like the taste of meat, and find that they feel a great deal better following a diet that is based on vegetables, pulses, grains and nuts.

Not only does the vegetarian diet satisfy the senses of taste and sight; it is very very good for you too. All the proteins needed for health are contained in beans, nuts, grains and dairy foods, and fruit and vegetables are just bursting with vitamins, wrapped up in wonderful flavour. But the question asked by most new vegetarians is what do we eat instead of meat? The answer is to include a much wider range of foods in our diet, rather than trying to replace meat or fish with another single item. Base each day's meals around beans and grains such as rice or pasta. Add eggs, nuts and cheese occasionally and serve plenty of vegetables and fruit at each meal.

It has to be said that vegetarian cooking does need a little thought – particularly if you are new to vegetarian recipes. Flavourings and seasonings become very important, and we have to plan ahead a little more carefully than with a meat-based meal. I hope that the recipes and ideas in this book will help to make your vegetarian cooking easier and more enjoyable.

Kitchen Equipment

Virtually no special pieces of equipment are necessary for the preparation of vegetarian dishes. However, it does add to the pleasure and ease of cooking if the utensils you use are of good quality and kept in efficient working order. There is nothing more frustrating than to struggle with a worn-out grater or to try chopping parsley with a knife that does not quite meet the board. The following equipment will meet just about all the needs of an aspiring vegetarian chef, and should indeed be the basis of any sensible cook's kitchen.

• A solid wooden chopping board, a heavy straight-bladed cook's knife and a small sharp vegetable knife will cope with most cutting jobs. A serrated knife for cutting fruit is helpful too.
• A pair of kitchen scissors for snipping chives and small quantities of parsley. (Keep them well hidden though; handy for you means handy for everyone else too!)
• The skins of many vegetables like carrots and potatoes are rich in vitamins so the peel should be left on whenever possible. To this end a little stiff scrubbing brush will enable you to clean them quickly and efficiently without removing the skins and losing the vitamins.
• A good quality square grater is almost as quick to use as a food processor, especially for small quantities (and is certainly easier to clean!) A liquidizer, however, is invaluable for taking all the hard work out of soup making, and it will produce breadcrumbs in seconds.
• Freshly ground black pepper is an essential ingredient in all savoury recipes. Ready-ground pepper will not supply the same fresh pungency. Do invest in a good pepper mill, a medium-sized one is best so that you will have to refill it fairly frequently with freshly-bought peppercorns. Like all spices, peppercorns should not be stored for more than 2 months as they lose their flavour.
• A wok is best for stir-frying vegetables. Provided the vegetables are a similar size they cook rapidly and evenly, making sure that all the vitamins are retained. The food can even be served from the wok at the table

while it is still crisp and piping hot.

● A large frying pan with a lid means that cooking can often be completed on top of the cooker without having to use the oven.

● Food mixers are essential only if you make cakes very frequently. An electric handwhisk however is a boon for whisking small quantities of egg white and for magically smoothing a lumpy sauce.

● Herbs and spices are such an essential part of vegetarian cooking that a pestle and mortar soon becomes an invaluable kitchen tool! It's good for crushing garlic too.

● A deep-fat or sugar thermometer is less essential but very useful. It takes the guesswork out of preheating oil to the right temperature; one at which it will seal foods instantly without soaking in and making them greasy. It is also useful for boiling sugar when making ice creams and sweets.

A Guide to Buying

Delicious vegetarian dishes begin with the marketing. Because most recipes need only a minimum of cooking the basic raw ingredients should be of the best quality. Buy *fruit and vegetables* fresh each day if possible, choosing them carefully. Remember also to make full use of the unusual exotic fruits on sale in many supermarkets. They are especially welcome during the winter months while we wait for our own summer soft fruits and autumn plums and blackberries. Most of these fruits are shipped very under-ripe so if possible ask for the guidance of a greengrocer or shop assistant when selecting fruit, especially *pawpaw* and *kiwi fruit*. *Passion fruit* are easier, as their wrinkled appearance indicates ripeness. *Feijoa fruit* have a delicous almost perfumed flavour and a taste that is something between a pineapple and strawberry. The skin is pale green. Be sure to buy fully ripe.

When *fresh herbs* are plentiful, varied and comparatively cheap, buy larger bunches and wash, chop and freeze them in labelled containers. It will be a delight to have fresh basil, marjoram, mint and parsley in frosty December. Vary the vegetables and herbs specified in these recipes according to season.

Freshly-made plain and wholemeal pasta is available nowadays in many large supermarkets. It keeps well for 3-4 days covered in the refrigerator and cooks in a very short time. Try the Mushroom sauce on page 27 with fresh tagliatelle, quite delicious!

Brown rice and *dried wholewheat pasta* are good store-cupboard standbys. Either of these cooked, tossed in oil and combined with eggs, vegetables, cheese or a sauce from the freezer makes a quick and imaginative meal.

Shelled nuts become stale fairly quickly so if bought loose these should be from a shop with a rapid turnover. If wrapped they should be well within their sell-by date. The same applies to spices and dried herbs. Buy only in small quantities and replenish supplies often. Dried herbs and spices should always be stored away from direct light in an airtight container, otherwise they will quickly lose their colour and flavour.

Dried beans, lentils and *peas* also do not keep indefinitely, so these too should be bought from a busy shop in fairly small quantities. The fresher they are the shorter time they will take to cook. Keep a few cans of cooked beans and chick peas in stock for emergencies. They are also useful if you have forgotten to soak the dried variety in advance.

Most recipes in this book use *wholemeal flour* or a combination of wholemeal and white flour. In case you are confused about it, wholemeal and wholewheat are the same thing. However, both 100% stoneground wholemeal and 81% wheatmeal are available. The latter has had part of the bran and wheatgerm removed and will need a little less water for mixing. Use whichever one is most readily available.

Sesame seeds, pumpkin seeds and *sunflower seeds* all add crunchy texture and extra food value to vegetarian dishes. They are all available in health food shops, as are *pine nuts* which, though expensive, add a wonderfully luxurious touch.

Agar agar is also to be found in health food shops. It is used instead of gelatine (which is made from hooves and bones). Made from seaweed, agar agar dissolves in boiling water and will set jellies and savoury mousses.

Speeding Things Up

Stock

When you have time to spare make homemade stock to keep in the freezer (see page 13). As an alternative, vegetable stock pastes and cubes are available in health food shops which can be added to boiling water for instant stock. Add salt with care to dishes that include commercial stocks as they can be very salty. Yeast extract, soy sauce, tomato purée and mushroom ketchup may all be used as quick stocks. Vary the quantities to suit recipe and taste.

Fresh Herbs

Fresh herbs are essential to vegetarian cooking; they can transform the simplest meal into a delight. If you can, keep the corner of the garden nearest to the kitchen door just for herbs and simply let them spread. A window box is large enough to grow a useful selection of herbs; parsley is usually easy to buy (and difficult to grow) so concentrate on chives, dill, rosemary, mint, basil and thyme. Just pick a handful as needed to chop and use immediately. Freeze some of the excess in the summer and keep 'loose' in the freezer, or blend some into butter and freeze ready for herb bread or to serve on top of steamed vegetables.

Breadcrumbs

Keep a plastic container of fresh wholemeal breadcrumbs in the freezer. Use as a quick crunchy topping for gratins, Stuffed Mediterranean vegetables (page 39) or for Blackberry and almond flan (page 71).

Rice

Cooked rice keeps perfectly for up to 2 days in the refrigerator in an airtight plastic container. Use for recipes such as Tropical salad (page 64).

Beans

Cooked beans also keep well for up to 2 days in an airtight plastic container in the refrigerator.

Sauces

When making sauces prepare twice the amount and freeze some for use when time is short. Rich tomato sauce (page 46) or Mushroom sauce (page 27) are especially suitable for this.

Light French Dressing

Always have a screw-top jar of dressing ready in the refrigerator for serving with salads.

Nuts

Keep a variety of nuts ready chopped in sealed plastic containers. They will keep well for up to 2 weeks.

Soaking and cooking beans

Canned chick peas and red kidney beans are practical when only small quantities are needed. However, for those who prefer to soak and cook beans from dried remember that it's always wise if you have time to soak beans overnight before using. This helps them to cook more quickly and makes them more digestible. Rinse the beans well after soaking and again after cooking. Do not add salt to the cooking water as it tends to toughen the skins.

Safe Red Kidney Beans

Uncooked red kidney beans contain a toxin which is harmful. In order to destroy this it is essential that the beans are properly cooked following this method:
1. Cover the beans with cold water and soak overnight.
2. Rinse the beans under cold running water. Put the beans in a pan, cover with water and bring to the boil.
3. *Boil vigorously for 20 minutes* then lower the heat, cover the pan and simmer for 1-1¼ hours until tender.
4. Drain and rinse thoroughly. The beans are now properly cooked and ready for use.

Meal planning

Choosing a balanced combination of dishes, without the traditional focal point of meat or fish, can be a problem at first. The basic principle of trying to achieve contrast in flavour, texture and colour still stands, but in the beginning it's important to make sure that the overall meal doesn't contain too many stodgy elements (pastry, rice or pasta), too many vegetable or fruit based courses, or is too rich in dairy produce. With practice, achieving an imaginative, nutritious and satisfying selection of dishes becomes almost second nature, but to aid the process, here are a few ready-planned meal suggestions:

INFORMAL DINNER PARTIES OR FAMILY MEALS

1. Cheese Granary Toasts.
   Mixed Salad Choice.
   Plum Cheesecake.

2. Smoked Cheese and
   Nut Salad.
   Winter Stew with
   Dumplings.
   Colcannon.
   Cranachan with Fruit
   Kissel.

3. Nut Stuffed Tomatoes.
   Crumbly Nut Roast.
   Summer Vegetables with
   Yogurt and Mint.
   Kartoshki.
   Cider Pears with
   Passionfruit.

4. Spinach Soup.
   Family Vegetable Pie.
   Braised Onions in Cider
   and Sage.
   Apricot and Orange
   Sorbet.

5. Spinach and Cheese
   Lasagne.
   Fruit and Vegetable
   Kebabs.
   Blackberry and Almond
   Flan.

6. Cheese and Celery
   Pâté.
   Hot Boston Beans.
   Leek, Potato and
   Coriander Bake.
   Winter Rhubarb Jellies.

DINNER PARTY MENUS

7. Courgette and
   Watercress Flan.
   Carrot and Apple Salad.
   Beansprout, Celery and
   Lancashire Cheese Salad.
   Hot Mustard Rolls.
   Strawberry Yogurt Ice.

8. Fennel with Walnuts.
   Roulade with Wine and
   Mushroom Filling.
   Lemon Cabbage with
   Poppy Seeds.
   Hot Garlic Bread.
   Melon and Raspberries in
   Sauternes.

QUICK MENUS

9. Tropical Fruits in
   Sherry.
   Tagliatelle with Cheese
   and Walnuts.
   Spinach, Chicory and
   Mushroom Salad.
   Fig and Honey Custard
   Tart
   (prepared in advance).

10. Mushroom Pâté
    (prepared in advance).
    Egg and Beansprout
    Tacos.
    Green and Gold Salad.
    Little Marzipan and
    Apple Pies
    (prepared in advance).

◆ S·O·U·P·S ◆

SPINACH SOUP

750g (1½lb) fresh spinach, washed thoroughly and stalks removed
25g (1oz) butter
1 small onion, peeled and finely chopped
25g (1oz) plain flour
600ml (1 pint) vegetable stock
about 300ml (½ pint) milk
salt

freshly ground black pepper
freshly grated nutmeg
To garnish:
about 2 tablespoons plain unsweetened yogurt
4 lemon slices (optional)

Preparation time: *30 minutes*
Cooking time: *20 minutes*

If fresh spinach is not available use a 275g (10oz) pack of frozen spinach instead. Spinach should be cooked for the shortest possible time to retain its colour and nutritional value, so for this soup it is cooked separately. No water is necessary, as spinach contains a high proportion of water.
1. Cook the spinach without water in a covered pan for 6-8 minutes, then turn into a bowl. (Heat frozen spinach just until thawed.)
2. Rinse out the pan and melt the butter in it. Add the chopped onion, fry gently without browning for 5 minutes then add the flour. Cook for 3 minutes, then pour in the stock. Stir well, bring to the boil and simmer for 3-4 minutes.
3. Cool slightly, then pour into a liquidizer or food processor, add the cooked spinach and blend until smooth.
4. Pour back into the pan and stir in sufficient milk to give a pouring consistency.
5. Add salt, pepper and nutmeg to taste. ⅌ Reheat and serve, garnishing each bowl with a swirl of yogurt and a slice of lemon, if liked.
⅌ Can be frozen in a plastic container for up to 6 weeks. Thaw overnight at room temperature and reheat gently.

CARROT AND LENTIL SOUP

25g (1oz) butter
1 medium onion, peeled and chopped
1 clove garlic, peeled and crushed (optional)
2 carrots, about 100g (4oz), scrubbed and chopped
2 sticks celery, trimmed, scrubbed and chopped
150g (5oz) red lentils, washed and drained
1 litre (1¾ pints) vegetable stock
salt

freshly ground black pepper
2 teaspoons lemon juice
about 150ml (5fl oz) milk
2 tablespoons chopped fresh parsley
Croûtons:
oil, for shallow frying
4 slices wholemeal bread, crusts removed and cut into 1cm (½ inch) cubes

Preparation time: *20 minutes*
Cooking time: *45 minutes*

Few things are as comforting as a bowl of hot homemade soup. This one freezes well so it is a good one to make in advance ready to thaw and reheat. Served with Hot garlic bread (page 65) and fresh fruit it makes a nourishing meal.
1. Melt the butter in a large pan and fry the onion and garlic for 5 minutes until soft but not brown.
2. Add the carrots, celery and lentils and stir around in the butter for a few minutes. Pour in the stock, half cover the pan and simmer very gently for about 40 minutes, stirring occasionally.
3. Pour the soup into a liquidizer or food processor and blend until smooth. Pour back into the saucepan and season with salt and pepper. Add the lemon juice and thin the soup with milk to the consistency you prefer.
4. Taste and adjust the seasoning. ⅌ Stir in the parsley.
5. Keep the soup just simmering while you make the croûtons. Heat a little oil in a frying pan and fry the bread cubes in 2 batches until golden brown. Drain on kitchen paper.
6. Serve the soup piping hot in individual bowls, sprinkling with the croûtons at the last moment.
⅌ Can be frozen in a plastic container for up to 6 weeks. Thaw overnight at room temperature and reheat gently, then stir in the parsley.

FROM THE TOP Spinach soup; Carrot and lentil soup

LIGHT VEGETABLE SOUP

1 knob butter	1 teaspoon tomato purée
1 small onion, peeled and finely chopped	celery leaves
175 g (6 oz) carrots, scrubbed and cut into narrow matchstick strips	2 tablespoons chopped fresh parsley
	Omelette garnish:
3 sticks celery, trimmed, scrubbed and finely sliced	2 eggs
1 teaspoon cornflour	salt
900 ml (1½ pints) Homemade vegetable stock (see recipe right)	freshly ground black pepper
	15 g (½ oz) butter

Preparation time: *30 minutes*
Cooking time: *30 minutes*

For this delicate but surprisingly filling soup use homemade vegetable stock if possible.

1. Melt the butter in a large pan and fry the onion gently without browning for about 5 minutes.

2. Add the carrots and celery, cover the pan and cook gently for a few minutes more until the butter is absorbed.

3. Stir in the cornflour then add the stock and tomato purée. Bring to the boil, half cover the pan and simmer for about 20 minutes until the vegetables are crisply tender. [F]

4. Meanwhile make the omelette. Beat the eggs with the salt and pepper. Melt the butter in a small frying pan, add the beaten eggs and fry until set and very pale brown on the underside. Turn the omelette over and brown the other side. Slide on to a plate and cut into 1 cm (½ inch) dice.

5. Taste the soup and season with pepper and a little salt if needed. Stir in the chopped parsley.

6. Serve in individual bowls garnished with a few pieces of the omelette and a celery leaf.

[F] Can be frozen in a plastic container for up to 6 weeks. Thaw overnight at room temperature and reheat gently.

MUSHROOM AND HAZELNUT SOUP

25 g (1 oz) butter	450 ml (¾ pint) milk
350 g (12 oz) mushrooms, sliced	¼ teaspoon grated nutmeg
	salt
25 g (1 oz) ground hazelnuts	freshly ground black pepper
450 ml (¾ pint) vegetable stock	3 tablespoons single cream

Preparation time: *15 minutes*
Cooking time: *20 minutes*

FROM THE TOP Light vegetable soup; Mushroom and hazelnut soup

Hazelnuts give this soup a distinctive flavour and thicken it too. Good for a dinner party.

1. Melt the butter in a large pan, add the mushrooms and stir over a medium heat for 2-3 minutes until the juices run. Put the lid on the pan and simmer gently in the juices for 5 minutes. Take out 2 tablespoons of the mushrooms and reserve for garnishing later.

2. Stir in the hazelnuts, then add the stock, milk, nutmeg, salt and pepper. Cover the pan and simmer gently for 10 minutes.

3. Blend the soup in a liquidizer or food processor until smooth. Return to the rinsed-out pan, stir in the cream and the reserved cooked mushrooms and gently reheat until piping hot but not boiling.

4. Check and adjust the seasoning if necessary. Serve immediately.

HOMEMADE VEGETABLE STOCK

Makes about 1.75 litres (3 pints)	
1 tablespoon vegetable oil	3 sticks celery, scrubbed, trimmed and cut into chunks
2 medium onions, about 350 g (12 oz), peeled and quartered	1 teaspoon tomato purée
	6 black peppercorns
4 large carrots, about 450 g (1 lb), scrubbed and cut into chunks	1 teaspoon salt
	2.25 litres (4 pints) water

Preparation time: *10 minutes*
Cooking time: *2 hours*

Homemade stock makes all the difference to vegetarian recipes. It takes only minutes to prepare and can then be left to simmer away with no further attention. Keep the salt to a minimum and never add green leafy vegetables like cabbage as they spoil the background flavour. Brown the vegetables well at the start and the stock will be a good golden colour and the flavour rich and full. This is a large enough quantity to leave some for freezing.

1. Heat half the oil in a very large saucepan with a lid and fry the onion until quite dark brown. Remove and reserve. Add the remaining oil and brown the carrots, remove and reserve, then brown the celery.

2. Put all the vegetables back into the pan and add the tomato purée, peppercorns, salt and water.

3. Bring to the boil, stirring at first, so that the colour from the bottom of the pan is mixed into the stock. Cover and simmer on the lowest possible heat for about 2 hours.

4. Strain the stock and leave to cool. [A] [F]

[A] The stock can be prepared up to 3 days in advance and stored in the refrigerator.

[F] The stock can be frozen for up to 1 month. Freeze in 600 ml (1 pint) rigid containers, leaving headspace in the container.

ARTICHOKE SOUP

25 g (1 oz) butter

1 small onion, peeled and thinly sliced

450 g (1 lb) Jerusalem artichokes, scrubbed and sliced

salt

freshly ground black pepper

600 ml (1 pint) milk

300 ml (½ pint) vegetable stock

chopped fresh chives, to garnish (optional)

Preparation time: *15 minutes*
Cooking time: *30 minutes*

1. Melt the butter in a large pan and fry the onion gently without browning for about 5 minutes.

2. Add the artichokes, cover and cook for another 5 minutes so that the artichokes absorb the butter.

3. Add salt and pepper then pour in the milk and stock. Bring to the boil and simmer gently, half covered, for about 20 minutes until the artichokes are tender.

4. Blend in a liquidizer or food processor until smooth. Return the soup to the pan and reheat gently.

5. Taste and adjust the seasoning. Serve piping hot, sprinkled with chives (if liked) and Sesame Croûtons (see below).

SESAME CROÛTONS

Cut the crusts from 4 slices of brown bread. Dip each slice into beaten egg seasoned with salt and pepper and then into sesame seeds, coating both sides. Cut the dipped slices into squares, then cut each square into 2 triangles. Fry in shallow hot oil for about 30 seconds. Lift out with a slotted spoon and drain on paper towels.

LEEK AND POTATO SOUP

1 tablespooon vegetable oil	900 ml (1 ½ pints) vegetable stock
15 g (½ oz) butter	
1 small onion, peeled and thinly sliced	salt
	freshly ground black pepper
1 large leek, about 225 g (8 oz) washed and sliced	1 bay leaf
	2 tablespoons chopped fresh parsley
350 g (12 oz) potatoes, peeled and cut into 5 mm (¼ inch) cubes	

Preparation time: 15 minutes
Cooking time: 20 minutes

This soup, perfect for a cold winter's day, is best not liquidized. It is particularly good with warm Fresh herb scones (see next recipe).

1. Heat the oil and butter in a large pan and gently fry the onion for 3-4 minutes without browning.
2. Add the leek and potatoes, stir well then cover the pan and leave over a low heat for a few minutes until the butter and oil are absorbed.
3. Pour in the vegetable stock and add a little salt, plenty of black pepper and the bay leaf.
4. Cover the pan again, bring to the boil and simmer gently for about 15 minutes. Take care not to overcook.
5. Test to make sure the potato is tender, then taste and adjust the seasoning and remove the bay leaf.
6. Stir in the chopped parsley and serve piping hot.

FRESH HERB SCONES

Makes 8 scones	2 tablespoons chopped fresh herbs (parsley, sage, thyme, rosemary) or 2 teaspoons mixed dried herbs
100 g (4 oz) wholemeal self-raising flour	
100 g (4 oz) white self-raising flour	
	120 ml (4 fl oz) milk
½ teaspoon salt	1 tablespoon vegetable oil
freshly ground black pepper	milk, for brushing
50 g (2 oz) hard vegetable margarine	paprika, to garnish

Preparation time: 15 minutes, plus resting
Cooking time: 20 minutes
Oven: 220°C, 425°F, Gas Mark 7

These tasty scones can be ready to eat in about half an hour and are just right to serve warm with hot soup. They are good spread with unsalted butter too, for a tea-time snack.
1. Mix together the flours, salt and pepper in a bowl.
2. Rub in the margarine until the mixture resembles fine breadcrumbs, then mix in the herbs.
3. Make a well in the centre and slowly pour in the milk and oil, mixing lightly with a round-bladed knife to produce a soft dough.
4. Turn the dough on to a lightly floured surface and shape it into a ball, then flatten it gently with the palm of your hand to make a round about 15 cm (6 inches) across and 2½ cm (1 inch) thick.
5. Divide the round into 8 sections with a knife, cutting only halfway through the dough. Brush the top with milk and place on a floured baking sheet.
6. Leave to rest for 15 minutes in a warm place.
7. Bake near the top of the oven for about 20 minutes until well risen and golden brown. Remove from the oven and sprinkle with paprika.
8. Allow to cool on a wire tray. Ⓕ Break into sections to serve.
Ⓕ Can be frozen for up to 4 weeks. Thaw at room temperature and warm through in the oven before serving.

FROM THE LEFT Artichoke soup; Leek and potato soup; Fresh herb scones

·S·T·A·R·T·E·R·S·&·S·N·A·C·K·S·

POTATO JACKETS WITH SOURED CREAM DIP

5 large potatoes, scrubbed and dried
150 ml (5 fl oz) soured cream
1 teaspoon snipped fresh chives
salt
freshly ground black pepper
vegetable oil, for frying

Preparation time: *10 minutes*
Cooking time: *1½-1¾ hours*
Oven: *190°C, 375°F, Gas Mark 5*

These golden, crisp potato skins are an American speciality. The amounts given are plenty for four but an extra potato jacket or two is usually welcomed. Use the insides of the potatoes for Colcannon (page 58) or as a topping for a vegetable pie.
1. Prick the potatoes with a fork and bake for about 1¼ hours until tender; really large potatoes will take about 30 minutes longer.
2. Meanwhile prepare the dip. Mix the soured cream with the chives and salt and pepper to taste. Spoon into a bowl, cover and leave to chill in the refrigerator.
3. When the potatoes are cooked, leave to cool for a few minutes then cut each one lengthways into 4.
4. Using a teaspoon scoop out most of the potato leaving just a thin layer next to the skin. Ⓐ
5. Pour vegetable oil into a small pan to a depth of 7.5 cm (3 inches). There is no need to use a large deep-frying pan.
6. Heat the oil to 180°-190°C/350°-375°F or until a cube of bread browns in 30 seconds.
7. Fry 4-5 potato skins at a time for about 2 minutes until brown and crisp. Lift from the oil with a slotted spoon and drain on kitchen paper. Keep the skins hot in the oven while the remaining skins are cooked.
8. Either sprinkle the skins lightly with salt or provide salt for guests to help themselves. Serve with the chilled dip.
Ⓐ The uncooked potato jackets can be prepared up to 24 hours in advance. Cover and chill until required.

SMOKED CHEESE AND NUT SALAD

Serves 6
Nut dressing
50 g (2 oz) hazelnuts, coarsely chopped
6 tablespoons vegetable oil
2 tablespoons wine vinegar
salt
freshly ground black pepper
pinch of cayenne pepper
½ teaspoon made English mustard
½ teaspoon sugar

Salad:
1 crisp lettuce, shredded
1 head radicchio, separated into leaves
2 apples
1 tablespoon lemon juice
150 g (5 oz) German smoked cheese, cut into 1 cm (½ inch) cubes
1 bunch watercress, to garnish

Preparation time: *15 minutes*

An unusual colourful starter using radicchio. The same quantities will serve 2-3 as a main meal salad.
1. First make the dressing. Toast the chopped hazelnuts under a medium grill until evenly browned. Cool.
2. Put all the remaining dressing ingredients into a screwtop jar, add the hazelnuts and shake for 1 minute until well mixed.
3. Arrange the lettuce and radicchio on 6 individual plates. Cut the apples into 1 cm (½ inch) cubes, toss in the lemon juice and arrange with the cubes of cheese on top of the salad leaves.
4. Spoon the dressing over the cheese and apple just before serving.
5. Garnish with sprigs of watercress and serve.

FROM THE TOP Potato jackets with soured cream dip; Smoked cheese and nut salad

RAW WINTER VEGETABLES WITH SKORDALIA

Dip:	3 tablespoons chopped fresh parsley
300 ml (10 fl oz) low-calorie mayonnaise	
	2-4 tablespoons plain unsweetened yogurt (optional)
25 g (1 oz) fresh wholemeal breadcrumbs	
	Vegetables:
25 g (1 oz) ground almonds	about 175 g (6 oz) each of:
2 cloves garlic, peeled and crushed (or more if you like)	scrubbed celeriac, scrubbed carrot, white cabbage, red cabbage, trimmed broccoli,
salt	trimmed cauliflower, trimmed
freshly ground black pepper	Brussels sprouts, peeled onions
squeeze of lemon juice	
2 tablespoons sesame seeds, toasted	

Preparation time: *45 minutes*

Serve this Greek dip with some or all of the suggested raw vegetables. It makes a stunning starter for a party, and to serve 4 as a main meal, simply add a basket of Hot garlic bread (page 65). Remember that vegetables quickly lose their vitamins once cut, so choose very fresh crisp vegetables and prepare them only an hour or two before serving.
1. Make the dip. Put the mayonnaise into a bowl and stir in the breadcrumbs and almonds. Add the garlic, salt, pepper and lemon juice.
2. Now stir in the sesame seeds and parsley. If the mixture seems a little stiff, add plain unsweetened yogurt to give a softer consistency.
3. Taste and adjust the seasoning. Ⓐ Cover and set aside while you prepare the vegetables.
4. Grate the celeriac and carrot, shred the white and red cabbage and thinly slice the broccoli, cauliflower, Brussels sprouts and onions.
5. Serve clusters of the vegetables on a large platter or in small separate dishes, with the dip in the centre.
Ⓐ Skordalia can be made up to 2 hours in advance, covered and kept at room temperature.

AVOCADO AND STILTON TOASTS

4 slices wholemeal bread	75 g (3 oz) Blue Stilton cheese
15 g (½ oz) butter	To garnish:
1 large ripe avocado	8 small lettuce leaves
1 tablespoon lemon juice	sprigs of watercress
freshly ground black pepper	

Preparation time: *10 minutes*
Cooking time: *5 minutes*

Cut long slanting slices from a wholemeal French loaf for this simple but unusual starter. Danish blue cheese can be used instead of Blue Stilton if preferred.
1. Place the wholemeal bread under a preheated grill and toast on one side. Lightly butter the untoasted side.
2. Peel and halve the avocado, removing the stone. Cut into quarters, then slice each quarter into 4.
3. Arrange the slices of avocado on the buttered side of each piece of toast and sprinkle with lemon juice and pepper.
4. Cut the cheese into 4 thin slices and lay one over the avocado slices on each piece of toast.
5. Reduce the grill to medium and grill the toasts lightly until the cheese is melted.
6. Serve immediately garnished with the lettuce and sprigs of watercress.

CHEESE GRANARY TOASTS

Makes 8-12 toasts	225 g (8 oz) mature Cheddar cheese, grated
4 tablespoons milk	
25 g (1 oz) butter	salt (optional)
2 teaspoons malt vinegar	8-12 slices granary bread
freshly ground black pepper	To garnish:
large pinch of cayenne pepper	mustard and cress
	paprika
½ teaspoon made English mustard	

Preparation time: *15 minutes*
Cooking time: *5 minutes*

The very best and quickest snack I know, but be sure to use a really strong-tasting cheese. Keep a batch of this topping ready in the refrigerator.
1. Put the milk, butter, vinegar, pepper, cayenne and mustard into a pan.
2. Bring slowly to the boil then take off the heat and add the grated cheese immediately and all at once.
3. Beat thoroughly for a minute until the mixture is light and creamy. Taste and add a little salt if necessary. The topping is now ready to spread. Ⓐ
4. Toast the bread on one side only. Spread the untoasted side thickly with the topping and put back under the grill for 3-4 minutes until the topping is golden brown.
5. Cut in half and serve immediately garnished with mustard and cress and a sprinkling of paprika.
Ⓐ The topping can be kept covered in the refrigerator for up to 1 week. Bring back to room temperature to make it easier to spread.
Variation:
For a different taste and texture, stir 25 g (1 oz) chopped salted peanuts into the mixture before spreading on the bread (but do not add any salt to the mixture).

SPICY TOMATO CHICK PEAS

CLOCKWISE FROM TOP LEFT Raw winter vegetables with skordalia (in bowl); Spicy tomato chick peas; Avocado and stilton toasts

Serves 2

2 teaspoons vegetable oil	1 teaspoon tomato purée
1 onion, peeled and sliced	2 teaspoons sugar
½ teaspoon garam masala	salt
½ teaspoon ground cumin	freshly ground black pepper
¼ teaspoon ground chilli	1 green pepper, seeded and diced
dash of Tabasco sauce	
1 × 400g (14oz) can tomatoes	1 × 400g (14oz) can chick peas

Preparation time: *15 minutes*
Cooking time: *25-30 minutes*

A warming light supper for two, quickly prepared and cooked. Serve with plain brown rice and perhaps a bowl of crunchy raw fennel.

1. Heat the oil and fry the onion gently for 5 minutes. Stir in the garam masala, cumin, chilli and Tabasco sauce.

2. Pour in the tomatoes with their juice, tomato purée, sugar, salt and pepper. Simmer gently for about 4 minutes, then add the green pepper.

3. Continue simmering for a further 3-4 minutes until the sauce is smooth and thick. Ⓐ

4. Drain the chick peas and reserve 4 tablespoons of liquor. Stir the chick peas and liquor into the sauce and cook gently for 8-10 minutes to heat the chick peas, stirring occasionally.

5. Serve piping hot.

Ⓐ The sauce can be prepared up to 24 hours in advance and kept covered in the refrigerator.

CHEESE AND CELERY PÂTÉ

225 g (8 oz) low fat soft cheese	freshly ground black pepper
	dash of Tabasco sauce
2 sticks celery, scrubbed and finely chopped	To garnish:
	about 1 teaspoon crushed black peppercorns
2 spring onions, trimmed and finely chopped	2 teaspoons chopped fresh parsley
celery salt	

Preparation time: 15 minutes, plus chilling

A quickly made pâté that is best if chilled for 1-2 hours before serving to allow the flavours to mature. Serve with crusty granary bread or fingers of toast as an unusual appetizer.

1. Put the cheese, celery and spring onions in a bowl. Mix well and beat in the celery salt, pepper and Tabasco.
2. Spoon the pâté into a small serving dish. Garnish the top with alternate lines of chopped parsley and crushed peppercorns. Cover and chill in the refrigerator for 1-2 hours before serving. Ⓐ
Ⓐ May be chilled for up to 24 hours but cover with clingfilm to prevent the strong flavours from permeating other foods in the refrigerator.

◢TROPICAL FRUITS IN SHERRY

1 medium-sized ripe pawpaw (papaya)	150 ml (5 fl oz) medium or dry sherry
2 kiwi fruit	sprigs of fresh mint, to garnish
2 small bananas	
1 tablespoon lemon juice	

Preparation time: *10 minutes, plus marinating*

Unusual tropical fruits are now easy to find in most large stores. Pawpaw, added to more familiar tropical fruits and steeped in sherry, makes a fresh and colourful start to a special meal.

1. Using a sharp knife, peel the pawpaw, cut it in half and scrape out the black pips. Cut the flesh into long slices and put into a small bowl.
2. Peel the kiwi fruit, cut into slices and add to the bowl.
3. Skin the bananas and cut into slices. Put into another bowl and sprinkle with the lemon juice to stop them discolouring.
4. Now add the bananas to the other fruits and pour the sherry over them. Cover the bowl and leave to marinate for 2 hours in the refrigerator.
5. Spoon the fruits carefully into 4 glasses, adding a little of the sherry to each one.
6. Garnish with mint and serve.

◢FENNEL WITH WALNUTS

2 small fennel bulbs, with leaves	100 g (4 oz) walnuts, chopped
Dressing:	salt
4 tablespoons olive oil	freshly ground black pepper
1 clove garlic, peeled and crushed (optional)	

Preparation time: *10 minutes*
Cooking time: *1 minute*

Crisp aniseed-flavoured fennel smothered in hot walnut dressing is simply delicious and made in minutes.

1. Slice the fennel into thin, short strips, reserving the feathery leaves. Divide between 4 individual dishes.
2. Heat the olive oil in a small pan and add the garlic and walnuts. Fry quickly until the walnuts just begin to brown. Add salt and pepper then spoon the hot dressing over the cold fennel.
3. Garnish with the reserved fennel leaves and serve immediately.

◢COURGETTE FRITTERS WITH BLUE CHEESE DIP

5 small courgettes, about 275 g (10 oz)	vegetable oil, for frying
Batter:	Dip:
100 g (4 oz) wholemeal self-raising flour	4 tablespoons low-calorie mayonnaise
½ teaspoon salt	4 tablespoons plain unsweetened yogurt
freshly ground black pepper	50 g (2 oz) Danish Blue cheese, crumbled
1 egg	freshly ground black pepper
1 tablespoon vegetable oil	
2 teaspoons vinegar	
150 ml (5 fl oz) milk	

Preparation time: *30 minutes*
Cooking time: *20 minutes*
Oven: *110°C, 225°F, Gas Mark ¼*

Short sticks of celery or small florets of cauliflower may be used instead of courgettes and cooked in the same way.

1. Trim the courgettes and cut into short sticks about 5 cm (2 inches) long and 5 mm (¼ inch) wide. Dry on kitchen paper.
2. Make the batter. Put the flour, salt, pepper, egg, oil, vinegar and half the milk into a basin, whisk to a thick paste then gradually whisk in the rest of the milk. Ⓐ
3. Now prepare the dip. Blend the mayonnaise and yogurt together in a basin, fold in the cheese and season with plenty of pepper. Ⓐ
4. Pour vegetable oil into a small pan to a depth of about 7.5 cm (3 inches); there is no need to use a large deep frying pan. Heat the oil to 180°-190°C/350°-375°F or until a cube of bread browns in 30 seconds.
5. Dip each piece of courgette into the batter, allowing any excess to run back into the bowl, and then fry in small batches until puffy and golden (about 3 minutes per batch). Lift out with a slotted spoon, drain on kitchen paper, and keep hot on a serving dish in the preheated oven until you have completed the frying.
6. Sprinkle the fritters lightly with salt and serve hot with the Blue cheese dip.

Ⓐ The batter and dip can both be made up to 24 hours in advance and kept covered in the refrigerator.

CLOCKWISE FROM THE TOP Fennel with walnuts; Courgette fritters with blue cheese dip; Tropical fruits in sherry

SUGGESTED TOPPINGS FOR BLINI

a) Cottage cheese with radish and cress
b) Diced apple and celery mixed with yogurt
c) Soured cream with chopped pecan nuts
d) Mozzarella cheese with stuffed olives
e) Sliced tomatoes with soured cream
f) Diced cucumber with plain unsweetened yogurt

BLINI

Makes 16-20
100 g (4 oz) buckwheat flour or plain wholemeal flour
100 g (4 oz) plain white flour
½ teaspoon salt
2 teaspoons Easy Bake yeast
1 egg, separated

1 tablespoon vegetable oil
about 300 ml (½ pint) tepid milk
To serve:
a selection of toppings (see hint box)
sprigs of watercress, to garnish (optional)

Preparation time: 10 minutes, plus standing
Cooking time: 20 minutes

MUSHROOM PÂTÉ

50 g (2 oz) butter
2 shallots or small onions, peeled and finely sliced
1 clove garlic, peeled and crushed (optional)
225 g (8 oz) flat mushrooms, sliced
25 g (1 oz) fresh wholemeal breadcrumbs
100 g (4 oz) cottage cheese

large pinch of ground nutmeg
large pinch of ground mace
salt
freshly ground black pepper
25 g (1 oz) butter, melted
To serve:
1 tablespoon chopped fresh parsley, to garnish
lemon wedges

Preparation time: 15 minutes, plus chilling
Cooking time: 20 minutes

A useful vegetarian spread. Tasty with chopped watercress as a sandwich filling, or served with warm granary bread and butter.

1. Melt half the butter in a pan with a lid and fry the shallots or onions and garlic gently for 3 minutes. Add the mushrooms, cover the pan and cook for 15 minutes. Remove the lid, turn up the heat and reduce the liquid until the mushrooms are just moist. Melt the remaining butter.

2. Cool slightly then put the mushrooms with the breadcrumbs, cheese, nutmeg, mace, salt, pepper and butter in a liquidizer or food processor and blend until smooth.

3. Check and adjust the seasoning, and spoon the spread into a small dish. Cover and chill for 1-2 hours in the refrigerator. Ⓐ

4. Just before serving sprinkle the top with parsley. Serve with lemon wedges.

Ⓐ May be kept chilled for up to 36 hours, covered tightly with clingfilm to prevent the flavour permeating the other foods in the refrigerator.

Blini are little pancakes; a Russian version of Scotch pancakes. Buckwheat flour gives them a speckled dark colour and a distinct flavour but it is not always easy to find, so use wholemeal instead if necessary. Buckwheat flour will absorb less liquid than wholemeal so use slightly under the measure of milk to begin with, adding more if the batter seems too thick.

1. Put the flours, salt, yeast, egg yolk and oil into a bowl. Pour in the tepid milk and mix to thick smooth batter. Cover and leave to stand for 1 hour. The surface of the batter should be puffy and covered with bubbles.

2. Whisk the egg white and fold into the batter. The mixture is now ready for use.

3. Heat a lightly oiled griddle or frying pan over a steady heat. Drop 2 tablespoons of batter into the pan and cook for 3 minutes until tiny holes appear over the surface. Turn the pancake over and cook the other side for 2 minutes. Cook 3-4 blini at a time. When ready, keep warm between the layers of a clean teatowel, folded on a plate over boiling water.

4. To serve, arrange 2-3 warm blini with one or more of the chosen toppings on a small plate and garnish with sprigs of watercress if liked. Ⓐ

Ⓐ The blini may be made up to 8 hours in advance and gently reheated between the layers of a clean teatowel, folded on a plate over boiling water.

◢NUT STUFFED TOMATOES

Serves 2	
2 large Mediterranean tomatoes	25g (1 oz) brazil nuts, coarsely chopped
salt	25g (1 oz) currants
Stuffing:	1 teaspoon chopped fresh basil or ½ teaspoon dried basil
2 tablespoons vegetable oil	
75g (3 oz) button mushrooms, finely chopped	freshly ground black pepper
	To garnish:
65g (2½ oz) brown rice, cooked (¼ quantity Cooked brown rice page 42)	4 teaspoons soured cream
	watercress sprigs

Preparation time: *20 minutes*
Cooking time: *20 minutes*
Oven: *180°C, 350°F, Gas Mark 4*

As a starter these are delicious piping hot, but they are equally good uncooked; serve them with salad and French bread to make a light lunch for two.

1. Cut the tomatoes in half and scoop out the pulp. Sprinkle the shells with salt and place in a baking dish.

2. To prepare the stuffing, heat the oil in a small pan and gently fry the mushrooms for 5 minutes. Stir in the cooked rice, nuts, currants and basil. Add a little salt and plenty of pepper.

3. Spoon the stuffing into the tomato halves. Ⓐ

4. Cover the dish with foil to keep the stuffing moist and bake for 20 minutes in a preheated oven.

5. Remove from the oven, top each stuffed tomato with a spoonful of soured cream and garnish with watercress. Serve piping hot.

Ⓐ The tomatoes can be prepared up to 8 hours in advance, covered and kept in the refrigerator.

CLOCKWISE FROM THE LEFT Mushroom pâté; Blini with a selection of toppings, Nut stuffed tomatoes

·M·A·I·N· C·O·U·R·S·E·S·

MUNG BEAN AND FRESH HERB RISOTTO

175g (6oz) mung beans, soaked for 2 hours in cold water

15g (½oz) butter

1½ tablespoons vegetable oil

1 large onion, peeled and chopped

225g (8oz) long-grain brown rice

750ml (1¼ pints) hot vegetable stock

3 tablespoons chopped mixed fresh herbs (parsley, thyme, basil, mint)

salt

freshly ground black pepper

2 tablespoons pumpkin seeds

Preparation time: *15 minutes, plus soaking*
Cooking time: *about 50 minutes*

1. Drain and rinse the beans.
2. Using a large pan with a well-fitting lid, heat the butter and 1 tablespoon of the oil and fry the onion for 3 minutes, then stir in the beans and rice.
3. Pour on the hot stock and bring to the boil. Cover the pan, lower the heat and simmer gently for 40 minutes until beans and rice are tender and all the stock has been absorbed.
4. Add the herbs, salt and pepper and gently fork them through the mixture. Spoon the risotto into a warm serving dish and keep warm.
5. Fry the pumpkin seeds rapidly in the remaining oil for ½ minute (take care, as they jump about in the heat) then sprinkle over the risotto. Serve hot.

SAVOURY SANDWICH PUDDING

25g (1oz) butter

6 slices brown bread from a small loaf, crusts removed

100g (4oz) Cheddar cheese, grated

3 tomatoes, skinned and sliced

2 eggs

½ teaspoon made English mustard

salt

freshly ground black pepper

pinch of cayenne pepper

300ml (½ pint) milk

Preparation time: *20 minutes*
Cooking time: *45 minutes*
Oven: *180°C, 350°F, Gas Mark 4*

Accompanied by crisp green salad and followed by fresh fruit this would make a simple and satisfying meal.
1. Lightly oil a 900ml (1½ pint) pie dish.
2. Butter the bread and make 3 sandwiches using 75g (3oz) of the cheese and the tomatoes. Cut each one into 4 triangles and arrange in the dish.
3. Whisk together the eggs, mustard, salt, pepper, cayenne pepper and milk and gently pour over the sandwiches.
4. Sprinkle the remaining cheese on top and place near the top of the oven for about 45 minutes until puffed and golden.

TAGLIATELLE WITH CHEESE AND WALNUTS

Serves 3

salt

250g (9oz) fresh tagliatelle

100g (4oz) cream cheese

100g (4oz) soured cream

50g (2oz) walnuts, finely chopped

freshly ground black pepper

black grapes, halved and pips removed, to garnish

Preparation time: *10 minutes*
Cooking time: *10 minutes*

A lovely pasta dish which is ready to eat in minutes. It is almost as good made with dried pasta, but increase the cooking time of the pasta to about 8 minutes.
1. Bring a large pan of salted water to the boil and add the tagliatelle. Cook for about 3 minutes and then strain into a colander.
2. Put the cream cheese, soured cream and walnuts into the warm pan and stir over a low heat, adding a little salt and plenty of black pepper.
3. When the cheese and cream are beginning to melt, tip in the cooked tagliatelle and shake the pan to coat the pasta thoroughly.
4. Serve on warmed dishes, garnished with black grapes.

CLOKWISE FROM THE TOP Mung bean and fresh herb risotto; Tagliatelle with cheese and walnuts; Savoury sandwich pudding

HOT BOSTON BEANS

225 g (8 oz) haricot beans, soaked overnight in cold water
1 tablespoon vegetable oil
2 medium onions, peeled and chopped
4 tablespoons clear honey
3 tablespoons soy sauce
½ teaspoon Tabasco sauce
3 tablespoons wine vinegar
1 teaspoon English mustard powder
½-1 teaspoon ground chilli
1 teaspoon paprika
4 tablespoons tomato purée
450 ml (¾ pint) hot vegetable stock
4 tablespoons orange juice
2 teaspoons plain wholemeal flour
2 tablespoons water
2 red peppers, seeded and sliced

Preparation time: *20 minutes, plus soaking overnight*
Cooking time: *about 2¾ hours*
Oven: *150°C, 300°F, Gas Mark 2*

The ideal meal to come home to. Serve it with a dish of yogurt and cucumber salad and lots of hot garlic bread.
1. Rinse the beans and put in a pan with sufficient water to cover. Bring to the boil and simmer for 30 minutes. Drain and tip into a casserole.
2. Heat the oil in a large pan and gently fry the onions until golden. Stir in the honey, soy sauce, Tabasco sauce, vinegar, mustard, chilli, paprika and tomato purée.
3. Pour in the hot stock and orange juice and bring to the boil. Pour over the beans, cover the casserole and cook in the centre of the oven for 1½ hours.
4. Blend the flour with the water and stir into the beans. Add the red peppers.
5. Cover and return to the oven for 1 hour until the sauce is rich and thick and the beans tender. Ⓐ
6. Serve piping hot.
Ⓐ Can be prepared up to 24 hours in advance and kept covered and chilled. Reheat in the oven for about an hour.

MUSHROOM PASTA WITH PINE NUTS

1½ tablespoons vegetable oil	2 tablespoons double or whipping cream
1 medium onion, peeled and sliced	350 g (12 oz) pasta shapes (quills, spirals or cartwheels)
500 g (1¼ lb) flat open mushrooms, sliced	2 tablespoons pine nuts
salt	1 tablespoon chopped fresh parsley, to garnish
1-2 teaspoons green peppercorns	
1 tablespoon soy sauce	
3 tablespoons water	

Preparation time: *25 minutes*
Cooking time: *20 minutes*

This mushroom sauce has an unexciting appearance but a truly marvellous taste. Be sure to use the flat dark mushrooms; those freshly gathered from the field are best of all. Pine nuts, or pine kernels, are to be found in most health-food shops and delicatessens and are an important ingredient in this recipe.

1. Heat 1 tablespoon oil and fry the onion for about 5 minutes. Add the mushrooms and cook for a further few minutes until they have cooked down a little.
2. Add the salt, green peppercorns, soy sauce and water. Cover the pan and simmer gently for 20 minutes then remove the lid and cook quickly for about 1 minute to reduce some of the liquid.
3. Pour into a blender or food processor and blend very briefly, for just a few seconds (the mushrooms should retain some texture). Return to the rinsed-out pan and stir in the cream. Ⓐ Ⓕ
4. Prepare the pasta. Bring a large pan of salted water to the boil. Add the pasta, stir a couple of times and boil briskly for 10 minutes then drain thoroughly.
5. Meanwhile heat the remaining oil in a small pan and fry the pine nuts for ½ minute until golden brown. Drain on kitchen paper and set aside.
6. To serve, reheat the sauce without boiling and pour over the pasta. Sprinkle with the pine nuts and chopped parsley and serve immediately.

Ⓐ The sauce can be prepared up to 24 hours in advance and kept covered in the refrigerator.
Ⓕ The sauce can be frozen in a plastic container for up to 1 month. Thaw at room temperature before reheating very gently.

LEEK AND EGG PUFFS

Makes 4 puffs

Filling:	2 hard-boiled eggs, shelled and halved lengthways
1 medium leek, about 200 g (7 oz), washed and sliced	**Pastry:**
salt	225 g (8 oz) frozen and thawed puff pastry or Extra light pastry (see Family vegetable pie, page 30)
1 tablespoon vegetable oil	
1 small onion, peeled and thinly sliced	beaten egg, for glazing
freshly ground black pepper	
½ teaspoon coriander seeds, crushed	
50 g (2 oz) mature Cheddar cheese, cut into small cubes	

Preparation time: *30 minutes*
(or 45 minutes if making pastry)
Cooking time: *30 minutes*
Oven: *220°C, 425°F, Gas Mark 7*

Made with puff pastry, these are best eaten hot, but the wholewheat pastry version, with its moist filling, is excellent eaten cold, and makes a good picnic or packed lunch dish.

1. Cook the sliced leek in boiling salted water for 6 minutes, then strain and set aside.
2. Heat the oil in a small pan and fry the onion until golden brown. Add salt, pepper and coriander then stir in the cooked leek.
3. Allow the mixture to cool slightly and stir in the cheese.
4. Roll out the pastry thinly and trim to a 30 cm (12 inch) square. Cut it into four 10 cm (4 inch) squares. Cut the trimmings into leaf shapes to decorate the puffs.
5. Brush the edges of each pastry square with beaten egg. Divide the filling between the squares, placing it just off centre, and top with half a boiled egg. Fold the pastry over to make a triangle.
6. Seal the edges firmly and brush the tops with beaten egg. Arrange the pastry leaves on top and brush with beaten egg.
7. Bake for 15-20 minutes until puffed up and golden brown. Serve hot.

FROM THE TOP Mushroom pasta with pine nuts; Leek and egg puffs; Hot Boston beans

SPICED BROWN RICE WITH BROCCOLI

Serves 2

15 g (½ oz) butter	175 g (6 oz) broccoli, trimmed
1 medium onion, peeled and finely sliced	1 tablespoon olive oil
	50 g (2 oz) pine nuts
175 g (6 oz) long-grain brown rice	freshly ground black pepper
	salt
450 ml (¾ pint) vegetable stock	½ teaspoon garam masala (optional)

Preparation time: *20 minutes*
Cooking time: *30-40 minutes*

Although bright green broccoli looks attractive, several other vegetables could be used for this recipe; courgettes, mushrooms or peppers for instance. Pine nuts, which have a lovely creamy taste, are readily available in delicatessens and health-food shops. Thawed frozen broccoli can also be used instead of fresh.

1. Melt the butter and fry the onion until golden. Add the rice and fry gently for 2-3 minutes. Pour in the stock and bring to the boil, then cover the pan, lower the heat and simmer gently for 35-40 minutes until the rice is cooked but still slightly chewy, and all the stock has been absorbed.
2. About 15 minutes before the rice is cooked, prepare the broccoli. Cut the heads into thin strips lengthways, heat the olive oil in a large frying pan and stir-fry the broccoli for about 10 minutes. If you like the broccoli soft rather than slightly crisp, cover the pan for part of the time. This will create steam which will soften it further.
3. When the broccoli is cooked to taste add the pine nuts to the pan and stir-fry until they are lightly browned. Stir in the cooked rice, adding black pepper and a little salt if necessary (the stock may have provided enough salt).
4. Spoon into a serving dish, sprinkle lightly with garam masala (if liked) and serve immediately.

FROM THE LEFT Egg and beansprout tacos; Spiced brown rice with broccoli; Quick pan pizza

QUICK PAN PIZZA

Topping:	75g (3oz) white self-raising flour
1 tablespoon vegetable oil	
1 medium onion, peeled and thinly sliced	1/2 teaspoon mixed dried herbs
1 × 400g (14oz) can tomatoes	6 tablespoons water
	4 tablespoons vegetable oil
1 tablespoon tomato purée	To finish:
salt	100g (4oz) mature Cheddar cheese, sliced
freshly ground black pepper	
1 teaspoon sugar	6 stoned black olives
large pinch of cayenne pepper	1/2 teaspoon dried oregano
1 small green pepper, seeded and chopped	
Base:	
75g (3oz) wholemeal self-raising flour	

Preparation time: *35 minutes*
Cooking time: *30 minutes*

A super pizza prepared without using the oven. The rich tomato topping is covered with cheese and grilled to bubbling perfection in just a few minutes.

1. Prepare the topping. Heat the oil in a pan and gently fry the onion without browning for 7-10 minutes.
2. Add the tomatoes, tomato purée, salt, pepper, sugar and cayenne pepper. Break up the tomatoes a little with a wooden spoon and cook over a steady heat, stirring occasionally for 10 minutes. The mixture will thicken and reduce.
3. Stir in the green pepper and cook for a further 5 minutes. ▣
4. Prepare the base. Put the flours and 1/2 teaspoon salt into a bowl and mix in the dried herbs. Make a well in the centre and add the water and 2 tablespoons oil.
5. Mix to a fairly soft dough and turn on to a lightly floured surface. Knead gently into a ball and roll out to a round about 23cm (9 inches) in diameter to fit the base of a large frying pan.
6. Heat 1 tablespoon of the oil in the frying pan, lay the dough base of the pizza in it, and cook over a low heat for 8-10 minutes, lifting the edge now and again to see how it is getting on. When golden brown on the underside, lift it out and run the remaining tablespoon of oil into the pan. Replace the pizza cooked side uppermost and cook for a further 6-8 minutes.
7. Transfer the pizza base to an ovenproof plate (or leave it in the frying pan if the latter is suitable) and spread the topping over, right to the edge. Lay the cheese slices on top and place under a medium preheated grill for about 8 minutes until the cheese is melted and bubbly.
9. Garnish with olives and sprinkle with oregano. Serve hot with a crisp green salad.
▣ The topping may be prepared up to 36 hours in advance and kept tightly covered in the refrigerator.

YOGURT AND WATERCRESS DRESSING

150ml (5fl oz) plain unsweetened yogurt	1. Mix the yogurt in a bowl with the salt and pepper.
salt	2. Trim off most of the watercress stalks. Wash thoroughly and pat dry.
freshly ground black pepper	3. Chop fairly finely and stir into the yogurt.
1 bunch of watercress	4. Cover and leave at room temperature for 1 hour.

PREPARATION TIME:
5 minutes, plus standing

EGG AND BEANSPROUT TACOS

Serves 2-3	2 tablespoons chopped fresh parsley
6 taco shells	
2 tomatoes, sliced, to garnish	Filling 2:
Filling 1:	1 tablespoon olive oil
7 eggs	275g (10oz) beansprouts
3 tablespoons milk	1-2 tablespoons soy sauce
salt	
freshly ground black pepper	
15g (1/2 oz) butter	
2 tablespoons chopped capers	

Preparation time: *20 minutes*
Cooking time: *10 minutes*
Oven: *110°C, 225°F, Gas Mark 1/4*

Crisp taco shells stuffed with beansprouts and hot piquant scrambled eggs. Serves two, or even three, with a green side salad. Ready-to-use taco shells are widely available in supermarkets.

1. Warm the taco shells in the oven while preparing the fillings. Try to cook both fillings at the same time – they only take minutes.
2. Prepare Filling 1. Whisk the eggs, milk, salt and pepper together in a bowl. Melt the butter in a small pan and stir the eggs over a low heat to scramble them lightly. When almost ready stir in the capers and parsley.
3. Meanwhile make Filling 2. Heat the olive oil until smoking in a frying pan, add the beansprouts, and keeping the heat high, stir-fry for about 2 minutes, adding the soy sauce, some salt and plenty of black pepper.
4. Take the taco shells from the oven, spoon the beansprout filling in the bottom then top with the scrambled egg filling.
5. Garnish with slices of tomato and serve immediately.

FROM THE LEFT Soufflé lasagne; Family vegetable pie

◢FAMILY VEGETABLE PIE

Extra light pastry:

175 g (6 oz) wholemeal self-raising flour	100 g (4 oz) celery, scrubbed and sliced
salt	100 g (4 oz) cauliflower, cut into florets
1 teaspoon mixed dried herbs	about 300 ml (½ pint) milk
100 g (4 oz) hard vegetable margarine, from the freezer	25 g (1 oz) butter
3 tablespoons water	25 g (1 oz) plain flour
1 tablespoon vegetable oil	freshly ground black pepper
Filling:	2 tablespoons chopped fresh parsley
300 ml (½ pint) water	1 × 225 g (8 oz) can red kidney beans, drained
100 g (4 oz) carrots, scrubbed and sliced	beaten egg, for brushing
100 g (4 oz) leeks, washed and sliced	

Preparation time: *45 minutes, plus chilling*
Cooking time: *35 minutes*
Oven: *200°C, 400°F, Gas Mark 6*

This attractive and tasty pie is topped with a special, very light pastry. Remember to put the margarine into the freezer for an hour or two before you begin.

1. Put the flour, ¼ teaspoon salt and herbs into a bowl and grate the margarine into it. Mix lightly with a round-bladed knife to distribute the flakes of margarine, make a well in the centre and add the water and oil.

2. Mix gently to a firm dough, being careful not to over-handle it. Put the dough into a polythene bag and chill in the refrigerator while you make the filling. Ⓐ

3. Pour the water into a pan, add salt and bring to the boil. Put in the carrots, cover and simmer for 5 minutes then add the remaining vegetables, cover and cook for 10 minutes.

4. Strain the vegetables, reserving the liquid. Make this up to a generous 600 ml (1 pint) with milk. Melt the butter in the pan, add the flour and cook, stirring, for 3 minutes. Pour in the milk mixture and bring to the boil, stirring all the time, and simmer for 1 minute. Add salt and plenty of pepper then add the cooked vegetables, parsley and red beans. Pour into a 1.2 litre (2 pint) pie dish with a pie funnel in the centre.

5. Roll out the pastry into an oval 2.5 cm (1 inch) larger than the pie dish. Cut a strip off to cover the rim of the dish, brush with egg and place the lid in position. Trim and flute the edges. Cut any leftover pastry into decorations for the top of the pie. Brush with beaten egg, arrange the decorations on the pie and brush again with beaten egg.

6. Bake for 25 minutes until the pastry is golden brown.
Ⓐ The pastry can be prepared up to 24 hours in advance and kept chilled. Leave at room temperature for 20 minutes before rolling out.

PANCAKES WITH CARROT AND TAHINI FILLING

Pancake batter:

50 g (2 oz) buckwheat flour or plain wholemeal flour	10 g (¹/₄ oz) butter
50 g (2 oz) plain white flour	50 g (2 oz) cashew nuts
salt	450 g (1 lb) carrots, scrubbed and coarsely grated
freshly ground black pepper	275 g (10 oz) beansprouts
2 eggs, lightly beaten	freshly ground black pepper
3 tablespoons vegetable oil	1 tablespoon lemon juice
150 ml (5 fl oz) milk	4 tablespoons light tahini paste
150 ml (5 fl oz) water	1 tablespoon chopped fresh parsley

Filling:

1 tablespoon vegetable oil, plus extra for brushing

Preparation time: *45 minutes*
Cooking time: *25 minutes*
Oven: *220°C, 425°F, Gas Mark 7*

Tahini paste is made from sesame seeds and tastes a bit like peanut butter. I have used light tahini for this recipe, which is milder in flavour than the dark version, but both are available from health-food shops. Tahini combines well with carrots and together they make the basis of a very healthy filling for the pancakes. Both filling and pancakes can be made in advance and the two put together and warmed through in the oven. Yogurt and watercress dressing (see page 29) is a perfect accompaniment to this dish.

1. First make the pancakes. Put the flours, ¹/₂ teaspoon salt and pepper into a bowl. Add the eggs, 1 tablespoon oil and half the milk and mix to a smooth paste. Gradually whisk in the remaining milk and the water. Pour the batter into a jug.
2. Heat a teaspoon of oil in a small frying pan until smoking hot. Pour in about 2 tablespoons of batter, quickly tipping the pan so that it flows to the edges. Cook the pancake for 3 minutes then turn it over to cook the other side for about 1 minute.
3. Make 8 pancakes in this way, adding a little oil for each one. Keep them layered between sheets of kitchen paper until they are all cooked.
4. Now prepare the filling. Heat the oil and butter in a frying pan and fry the nuts for 2-3 minutes until browned. Add the grated carrots and cook for 3 minutes, stirring occasionally, then add the beansprouts and cook for a further 3 minutes.
5. Stir in the salt, pepper and lemon juice and finally add the tahini paste and parsley.
6. Spoon the filling on to the pancakes. Roll them up and place side by side in a lightly greased shallow dish. Brush with a little oil, cover the dish tightly with foil and heat in the oven for about 15 minutes. Serve piping hot.
Ⓐ The batter can be made up to 8 hours in advance and kept in the refrigerator until needed.

SOUFFLÉ LASAGNE

2 medium aubergines, about 450 g (1 lb), cut into 1 cm (¹/₂ inch) thick slices	freshly ground black pepper
salt	1 tablespoon chopped fresh basil or 1 teaspoon dried basil
150 g (5 oz) spinach lasagne (about 8 sheets)	Soufflé topping:
4 tablespoons vegetable oil	15 g (¹/₂ oz) butter
2 large onions, peeled and sliced	15 g (¹/₂ oz) plain flour
2 cloves garlic, peeled and crushed (optional)	300 ml (¹/₂ pint) milk
750 g (1 ¹/₂ lb) ripe tomatoes, skinned and sliced	2 eggs, separated

Preparation time: *45 minutes*
Cooking time: *about 1 hour*
Oven: *180°C, 350°F, Gas Mark 4*

This surprisingly light dish with its fluffy soufflé topping needs no accompaniment — just some granary bread to soak up the juices.

1. Sprinkle the aubergine slices with salt to draw out some of the excess liquid.
2. Cook the lasagne following the instructions for wholewheat lasagne on page 40, but reducing the cooking time to 10 minutes.
3. Heat 1 tablespoon of oil in a large frying pan and fry the onions and garlic for 5 minutes until soft but not brown. Spoon on to a dish and set aside.
4. Pat the aubergine slices dry with kitchen paper, heat 2 tablespoons of oil in the pan and fry half the slices on both sides until golden brown. Drain on kitchen paper and fry the rest of the aubergine in the remaining 2 tablespoons of oil.
5. Lightly oil a large shallow dish, about 2 litres (3¹/₂ pints) in capacity. Lay 4 lasagne sheets in the bottom, cover with a layer of aubergine then a layer of onion, then one of tomato. Sprinkle with salt, plenty of black pepper and half the basil. Repeat the layering once more, using all the remaining pasta, vegetables and herbs.
6. Now make the soufflé topping. Melt the butter in a small pan, stir in the flour and cook for 3 minutes. Pour in the milk, bring to the boil stirring all the time, season with salt and pepper and cook for 3 minutes until the sauce has thickened. Cool slightly then stir in the egg yolks.
7. Whisk the egg whites in a small bowl and fold them carefully into the sauce. Spoon the mixture into the dish, covering the top layer completely.
8. Bake for 45 minutes until the soufflé is risen and browned and serve piping hot.

ROULADE WITH WINE AND MUSHROOM FILLING

Filling:	Roulade:
2 teaspoons vegetable oil	5 eggs, separated
1 shallot or small onion, peeled and finely chopped	½ teaspoon made English mustard
225 g (8 oz) button mushrooms, chopped	1 teaspoon vinegar
150 ml (5 fl oz) dry white wine and vegetable stock mixed or 150 ml (5 fl oz) vegetable stock	100 g (4 oz) grated mature Cheddar cheese
	1 tablespoon grated Parmesan cheese
salt	
freshly ground black pepper	
3 tablespoons double or whipping cream	
1 bunch watercress, chopped, plus a few sprigs to garnish	

Preparation time: *30 minutes*
Cooking time: *20 minutes*
Oven: *200°C, 400°F, Gas Mark 6*

A roulade is really just a rolled-up soufflé omelette. This one, with a wine-flavoured mushroom filling, is impressive enough for a dinner party but quite easy to make. New potatoes with fennel and mint (page 48) and Broad beans with sesame (page 58) would complete the meal and make it one to remember.

1. Line a 23 × 33 cm (9 × 13 inch) Swiss roll tin with non-stick silicone paper or greased greaseproof paper.

2. First prepare the filling. Heat the oil in a pan with a lid and fry the shallot or onion for 5 minutes until tender but not brown. Add the mushrooms and cook for 2-3 minutes. Pour in the wine and stock and add a little salt and pepper.

3. Cover the pan and cook for about 5 minutes then remove the lid and boil rapidly to reduce the liquid to about 2 tablespoons. Stir in the cream and set aside while you make the roulade. Ⓐ

4. Whisk the egg yolks, salt, pepper, mustard and vinegar in a small bowl until light and thick. Fold in the grated Cheddar cheese.

5. In a large bowl whisk the egg whites until stiff. Take 2 tablespoons of the whisked whites and fold them into the cheese and yolk mixture to loosen it, then spoon it into the remaining whites and gently fold together until smoothly blended.

6. Pour the mixture into the prepared tin and gently smooth the surface. Bake near the top of the oven for 10-12 minutes until risen and golden brown. Remove from the oven but leave the oven on.

7. Sprinkle a sheet of greaseproof paper with Parmesan cheese and turn the roulade on to it. Peel off the silicone paper.

8. Gently reheat the mushroom filling mixture, but do not allow it to boil, and spoon it evenly over the roulade. Sprinkle the filling mixture with watercress, then roll the roulade up, just like a Swiss roll.

9. Lift carefully on to a warm serving dish and replace in the oven for about 4 minutes to heat through.

10. Serve piping hot, garnished with sprigs of watercress.
Ⓐ The filling can be prepared up to 8 hours in advance, tightly covered with clingfilm and left in the refrigerator. Reheat gently before using.

FRIED SPAGHETTI WITH FRESH HERBS

Serves 2	
150 g (5 oz) wholewheat spaghetti, broken into 10 cm (4 inch) lengths	2 hard-boiled eggs, shelled and coarsely chopped
salt	2 tablespoons chopped fresh mixed herbs (parsley, marjoram, thyme, mint)
1 tablespoon vegetable oil	
1 large onion, peeled and thinly sliced	
freshly ground black pepper	

Preparation time: *20 minutes*
Cooking time: *20 minutes*

An easy and undemanding pasta meal. The eggs complete the dish and the herbs give it colour and flavour. Very good served with a bowl of Onion and tomato sauce (see Popovers recipe on page 45).

1. Cook the spaghetti lengths in boiling salted water for 12

FROM THE LEFT Roulade with wine and mushroom filling; Crumbly nut roast

CRUMBLY NUT ROAST

40g (1½ oz) butter	175g (6oz) fresh wholemeal breadcrumbs
1 medium onion, peeled and chopped	salt
1 stick of celery, trimmed, scrubbed and chopped	freshly ground black pepper
225g (8oz) mixed nuts (walnuts, brazils and hazelnuts in equal quantities), coarsely chopped	1 teaspoon mixed dried herbs
	¼ teaspoon ground chilli
	2 eggs, lightly beaten
3 large tomatoes, about 225g (8oz), skinned and chopped	sprigs of watercress, to garnish

Preparation time: *30 minutes*
Cooking time: *50-60 minutes*
Oven: *220°C, 425°F, Gas Mark 7*

No vegetarian cook book would be complete without a nut loaf recipe. This one, moist and crumbly and packed with nourishment, is particularly good served with Rich brown gravy (see hint box), fresh noodles and a crisp green salad.

1. Oil a 450g (1lb) loaf tin and line the base with oiled greaseproof paper.
2. Melt the butter in a large pan and fry the onion and celery gently for 5 minutes without browning.
3. Add the nuts, tomatoes, breadcrumbs, salt, pepper, mixed herbs and chilli. Add the eggs and mix to a fairly soft consistency, then taste and adjust seasoning if necessary. Ⓐ
4. Spoon into the prepared tin, cover with oiled baking foil and bake for 50-60 minutes.
5. Ease off the foil and run a knife around the sides of the tin. Turn the loaf on to a warm dish and garnish with watercress.
Ⓐ The uncooked nut mixture can be prepared up to 8 hours in advance and kept covered.

minutes. Drain thoroughly.
2. Heat the oil in a large frying pan and fry the onions until golden.
3. Add the cooked spaghetti and fry for about 5 minutes until beginning to brown, turning over with a fish slice.
4. Add a little salt if necessary and plenty of pepper.
5. Add the eggs and herbs and lightly stir them through the spaghetti. Transfer to a warmed dish and serve.

RICH BROWN GRAVY

15g (½ oz) butter	as Crumbly nut roast (right).
15g (½ oz) plain flour	
450ml (¾ pint) hot water	1. Melt the butter in a small pan, add the flour and stir for 3 minutes over a fairly high heat until the flour turns golden brown.
1 teaspoon yeast extract	
1 teaspoon tomato purée	
1 tablespoon soy sauce	
freshly ground black pepper	2. Remove from the heat and pour in the water. Add the yeast extract, tomato purée, soy sauce and pepper.

PREPARATION TIME: *3-4 minutes*
COOKING TIME: *6 minutes*

Made in a few minutes, this lovely brown gravy will complement many vegetarian dishes such

3. Bring to the boil, still stirring, and simmer for 3-5 minutes until the gravy has reduced a little and is a nice rich brown. Pour into a jug and serve hot.

GOUGÈRE WITH RATATOUILLE

Choux pastry:	1 large aubergine, cut into
50 g (2 oz) hard vegetable margarine	2.5 cm (1 inch) cubes
	3 small courgettes, sliced
150 ml (5 fl oz) water	1 medium green pepper,
salt	seeded and diced
65 g (2½ oz) plain wholemeal flour	1 medium red pepper, seeded and diced
2 eggs (size 3), beaten	275 g (10 oz) tomatoes,
freshly ground black pepper	skinned, quartered and seeds
½ teaspoon made English mustard	removed
	2 tablespoons tomato purée
50 g (2 oz) mature Cheddar cheese, grated	1 teaspoon sugar
	1 tablespoon chopped fresh
1 tablespoon chopped fresh parsley, to garnish	basil or 1 teaspoon dried basil
Ratatouille filling:	
1 tablespoon vegetable oil	
1 large onion, peeled and coarsely chopped	

Preparation time: *50 minutes*
Cooking time: *about 40 minutes*
Oven: *220°C, 425°F, Gas Mark 7*

A satisfying dish which needs only a crisp green salad and a glass of red wine to complete the meal.

1. Make the pastry. Put the margarine, water and ¼ teaspoon salt in a large pan. Have the flour ready on a small plate nearby. Bring the margarine and water to a fast boil, draw the pan off the heat and tip in the flour all at once.

2. Beat briskly with a wooden spoon until the mixture forms a ball that rolls cleanly around the pan. Leave to cool for 5 minutes.

3. Slowly add the beaten egg, a little at a time, beating well between each addition. (An electric beater makes this job quick and easy.) When all the egg is incorporated, beat in plenty of black pepper, the mustard and the grated cheese.

4. Place adjoining heaped teaspoons of the mixture in a 25 cm (10 inch) circle on a greased baking tray, leaving rough peaks.

5. Bake in a preheated oven for about 40 minutes until the choux pastry is puffy and brown.

6. Meanwhile make the filling. Heat the oil in a pan and fry the onion gently without browning for about 10 minutes. Add the aubergine, courgettes, peppers and tomatoes. Stir in the tomato purée, sugar, basil, salt and pepper.

7. Cover the pan and simmer gently for a further 15 minutes, stirring once or twice during cooking. Ⓐ Ⓕ

8. Transfer the hot choux pastry ring to a heated platter and spoon in the ratatouille filling. Serve immediately, sprinkled with chopped parsley.

Ⓐ The ratatouille can be made up to 24 hours in advance, tightly covered in clingfilm and stored in the refrigerator.

Ⓕ The ratatouille can be frozen in a plastic container for up to one month. Thaw at room temperature before reheating gently in a saucepan.

RED PEPPER MACARONI CHEESE

175 g (6 oz) wholewheat macaroni	1 red pepper, seeded and cut into 1 cm (½ inch) dice
	2 tablespoons chopped fresh
salt	parsley (optional)
Sauce:	To garnish:
25 g (1 oz) butter	oil, for shallow frying
25 g (1 oz) plain white flour	3 thin slices wholemeal
750 ml (1¼ pints) milk	bread, cut into 12 triangles
freshly ground black pepper	
½ teaspoon made English mustard	
large pinch of cayenne pepper	
¼ teaspoon ground nutmeg	
225 g (8 oz) mature Cheddar cheese, grated	

Preparation time: *20 minutes*
Cooking time: *20 minutes*

It is important to use a good strong Cheddar for this homely dish. Leave out the red pepper if you prefer but it supplies contrast in colour, texture and flavour. Remember to reheat the sauce thoroughly after adding the macaroni, then all the dish needs is a few minutes under the grill.

1. Cook the macaroni in boiling salted water for about 15 minutes until just tender. Drain, rinse and set aside.

2. Now make the sauce. Using a pan large enough to accommodate the macaroni and sauce, melt the butter, add the flour and cook for 3 minutes, stirring. Pour in the milk and bring to the boil stirring all the time until the sauce thickens. Simmer for 3 minutes.

3. Add salt, pepper, mustard, cayenne and nutmeg, then stir in all but 25 g (1 oz) of the cheese.

4. Blanch the red pepper pieces in boiling water for 2 minutes then stir into the cheese sauce. Now add the cooked macaroni and reheat thoroughly but gently. Stir in the chopped parsley if using.

5. Either divide the mixture between 4 individual ovenproof dishes or put it into one large shallow ovenproof dish. Sprinkle with the remaining cheese and place under a medium grill for about 4 minutes to brown the top.

6. Meanwhile heat oil in a frying pan to a depth of 1 cm (½ inch) and fry the triangles of bread for a few seconds on both sides until golden brown. Drain on kitchen paper.

7. Take the macaroni cheese from the grill and arrange fried bread triangles around the edge of the dish(es).

FROM THE TOP Gougère with ratatouille; Red pepper macaroni cheese

STIR-FRY VEGETABLE RICE

Serves 3-4

1 ½ tablespoons olive oil	275 g (10 oz) long-grain brown rice, cooked (page 42), and dried (see below)
100 g (4 oz) carrots, scrubbed and cut into matchstick strips	
100 g (4 oz) small button mushrooms,. thinly sliced	2 tablespoons soy sauce
	salt
1 small green pepper, seeded and thinly sliced	freshly ground black pepper
3 spring onions, trimmed, peeled and finely sliced, plus 4 curled ones, to garnish (see hint box)	
50 g (2 oz) frozen peas	
4 eggs, beaten	

Preparation time: *20 minutes*
Cooking time: *about 15 minutes*

Cut the vegetables very finely and to roughly equal sizes, so that they cook quickly and evenly. It is very important that the cooked rice for this recipe should be dry, so spread it over 2 large plates and leave it in a warm place for about 15 minutes before using it.

1. Heat ½ tablespoon of the oil in a wok or large frying pan and stir-fry the carrots, mushrooms, pepper, spring onions and peas for about 3 minutes until lightly cooked but still crisp. Remove from the wok.

2. Heat another ½ tablespoon of oil in the wok, pour in the eggs and stir-fry until cooked and lightly brown, breaking them up into smallish pieces. Remove.

3. Add the remaining oil and stir-fry the dried cooked rice for 2 minutes. Add the soy sauce, a little salt and a generous amount of black pepper.

4. Return the vegetables and egg to the wok and stir all the ingredients gently together over a low heat. Serve piping hot, garnished with the curled spring onions.

CURLED SPRING ONIONS

Trim the roots and tops from the onions so that they are about 10 cm (4 inches) long. Make 3-4 vertical cuts in each onion, running through the green part down to within 2.5 cm (1 inch) of the base. Put the onions in iced water for about 30 minutes to 1 hour until curled. The onion tassels can be kept in the refrigerator for up to 8 hours.

FRITTATA

Serves 2

25g (1 oz) butter

4 eggs, beaten

275g (10oz) spinach, cooked and lightly chopped or 100g (4oz) frozen spinach, cooked

3 firm tomatoes, skinned and coarsely chopped

100g (4oz) cooked potatoes, diced or 75g (3oz) cooked brown rice

salt

freshly ground black pepper

1 teaspoon chopped fresh sage or ¼ teaspoon dried sage

few drops of Tabasco sauce

Preparation time: 15 minutes
Cooking time: 7 minutes

This is a thick, flat omelette cooked on both sides in the frying pan. It makes a substantial meal served with green salad and granary rolls. Good hot or cold, it is an excellent way of using up small quantities of left-over vegetables or rice. Other ingredients could be substituted for those suggested here.

1. Heat half the butter in a large frying pan until sizzling. Pour in the beaten eggs and stir for a few seconds.
2. Allow the eggs to settle in the pan and then distribute the spinach, tomatoes and potatoes or rice evenly over the surface.
3. Sprinkle with salt, pepper, sage and Tabasco sauce. Cook gently for about 4 minutes until the underside is set and golden brown. Gently lift the edge with a fish slice to check.
4. When the underside is done, tip the omelette out upside down on to a large plate, add the remaining butter to the pan, run it round over the heat to coat the base, then slide the omelette back into the pan and cook the other side for about 3 minutes.
5. Cut into quarters and serve hot or cold.

CRISP LENTIL PATTIES

Makes 8-10

225g (8oz) green or brown (Continental) lentils, washed and soaked overnight

450ml (¾ pint) vegetable stock

1 tablespoon oil

1 onion, peeled and finely sliced

1 green pepper, seeded and finely chopped

1 teaspoon ground cumin

1 teaspoon ground coriander

¼ teaspoon chilli powder

salt

freshly ground black pepper

100g (4oz) jumbo or porridge oats

1 egg, beaten

oil, for frying

watercress, to garnish

Preparation time: 20 minutes, plus soaking overnight
Cooking time: 50 minutes

Serve these spicy patties with the Onion and tomato sauce (see Popovers recipe on page 45) and tagliatelle or with a crunchy salad. Jumbo oats are easy to find in health food shops.

1. Rinse the lentils and put in a pan with the stock. Bring to the boil and simmer gently until all the stock is absorbed and the lentils are tender, about 40 minutes.
2. Meanwhile heat the oil in a pan and fry the onion slowly until cooked but not brown, about 10 minutes. Stir in the pepper and cook for a further 4 minutes then stir in the cumin, coriander, chilli powder, salt and pepper.
3. Add the lentils, mix well and leave to cool. Shape into round flat cakes.
4. Mix the oats with the salt on one plate and pour the beaten egg on to another. Dip each patty first into egg then into oats to coat completely. Ⓐ Ⓕ
5. Shallow fry the patties in oil for about 6 minutes, turning once, until brown and crisp. Drain on kitchen towels and keep hot.
6. Serve, garnished with watercress.
Ⓐ The uncooked patties may be prepared up to 8 hours in advance and kept tightly covered in clingfilm to prevent the flavours permeating the other foods in the refrigerator.
Ⓕ The uncooked patties can be frozen between layers of foil in a rigid plastic container. No need to thaw before frying but increase the cooking time to about 12 minutes.

FROM THE TOP Stir-fry vegetable rice; Spinach frittata; Crisp lentil patties shown with Beansprout, celery and Lancashire cheese salad (recipe page 63)

FROM THE LEFT Stuffed Mediterranean vegetables: Bean and pasta curry

BEAN AND PASTA CURRY

1 tablespoon vegetable oil	900 ml (1½ pints) vegetable stock
3 medium onions, peeled and chopped	1 tablespoon lemon juice
2 cloves garlic, peeled and crushed	salt (optional)
3 tablespoons curry powder	150 g (5 oz) pasta shapes (quills or twists)
½ teaspoon ground cumin	2 × 400 g (14 oz) cans red kidney beans
½ teaspoon ground coriander	
½ teaspoon ground chilli	
2 teaspoons grated fresh ginger (optional)	
2 tablespoons wholemeal flour	

Preparation time: *20 minutes*
Cooking time: *25 minutes*

Curry sauce improves with keeping and can be made the day before, and then simply reheated while the pasta cooks. Either way, a substantial meal can be made in about 45 minutes. Serve the curry with plain brown rice and some side dishes: quartered hard-boiled eggs, banana slices that have been sprinkled with lemon juice, cucumber slices and mango chutney.

1. Make the sauce. Heat the oil in a pan with a lid and fry the onion and garlic gently for 5 minutes. Stir in the curry powder, cumin, coriander, chilli, ginger and flour. Cook for 1 minute. Pour in the stock and lemon juice, bring to the boil, cover and simmer gently for 25 minutes. Taste and add salt if necessary. Ⓐ

2. Meanwhile prepare the pasta. Cook in plenty of boiling salted water for about 10 minutes until 'al dente'. Drain and rinse. Strain the kidney beans, reserving the liquor for thinning the sauce.

3. Add the pasta and beans, stirring them gently into the sauce. Thin down with the reserved bean liquor if necessary. Reheat and serve piping hot, with rice and a selection of accompaniments.

Ⓐ The curry sauce can be prepared 24 hours in advance, covered and kept in the refrigerator.

STUFFED MEDITERRANEAN VEGETABLES

2 medium aubergines	½ teaspoon yeast extract
2 large courgettes	salt
salt	freshly ground black pepper
2 large Mediterranean tomatoes (or 4 small ones)	¼ teaspoon cayenne pepper
	To garnish:
4 large flat field mushrooms (or 8 smaller ones)	2 teaspoons vegetable oil
	2 tablespoons pumpkin seeds
about 1 tablespoon vegetable oil, for brushing	1 tablespoon chopped fresh parsley
about 6 tablespoons water	
Stuffing:	
1 tablespoon vegetable oil	
1 clove garlic, peeled and crushed (optional)	
1 large onion, peeled and chopped	
100 g (4 oz) mushrooms, chopped	
200 g (7 oz) fresh wholemeal breadcrumbs	
2 teaspoons dried basil or 2 tablespoons chopped fresh basil	

Preparation time: *40 minutes*
Cooking time: *20-25 minutes*
Oven: *200°C, 400°F, Gas Mark 6*

This rich dark stuffing is used for a variety of vegetables, each of which contributes something to the overall flavour of the dish. Serve each person with a selection of different vegetables. The vegetables may also be cooked and served cold but not chilled.

1. First prepare the vegetables. Trim the aubergines and halve them lengthways. Hollow out the centres using a knife and a teaspoon. Cut the flesh into small pieces.
2. Prepare the courgettes in the same way. Sprinkle the aubergine and courgette pieces with salt and set aside. The salt will draw out some of the bitter juices.
3. Blanch the aubergine and courgette shells in boiling water for 2 minutes, then drain and set aside.
4. Cut the tomatoes in half and scoop the flesh and seeds into a bowl.
5. Trim the stalks from the field mushrooms and reserve.
6. Brush all the vegetable cases with oil, inside and out, and arrange in 2 roasting tins.
7. Now prepare the stuffing. Heat the oil in a pan and fry the garlic and onion for about 10 minutes until golden brown.
8. Chop the reserved mushroom stalks and add them together with the chopped mushrooms, breadcrumbs, basil, yeast extract, salt, pepper and cayenne.
9. Dry the aubergine and courgette pieces and add them to the pan with the flesh from the tomatoes.

10. Mix the stuffing thoroughly then spoon it into the prepared vegetable cases.
11. Pour 2-3 tablespoons of water into each roasting tin, place in the oven and bake for about 20 minutes until the vegetable cases are just tender.
12. While the vegetables are cooking prepare the garnish. Heat the oil in a small pan and fry the pumpkin seeds (take care as they will jump about) for 1-2 minutes until browned. Drain on kitchen paper, cool and mix with the parsley.
13. Lift the stuffed vegetables carefully on to a warm serving dish and sprinkle each one with pumpkin seeds and parsley.

RISOTTO MILANESE

50 g (2 oz) butter	175 g (6 oz) grated Parmesan cheese
1 onion, peeled and finely chopped	salt
350 g (12 oz) arborio rice (see below) or easy-cook long-grain Italian rice	freshly ground black pepper
150 ml (5 fl oz) dry white wine	
¼ teaspoon powdered saffron	
1.2 litres (2 pints) hot vegetable stock	

Preparation time: *5 minutes, plus standing*
Cooking time: *25 minutes*

This classic rice dish is excellent as an accompaniment to many vegetarian dishes, or as a meal on its own. Arborio rice is available at most delicatessens and large stores. Ordinary long-grain rice is almost as good, but the cooking time will be a little less.

1. Melt half the butter in a large pan, add the onion and fry gently for about 10 minutes until soft but not brown.
2. Add the rice and stir with a wooden spoon for 2-3 minutes then pour in the wine, increase the heat and cook quickly for a few minutes until it has reduced by half.
3. Dissolve the saffron in about 150 ml (5 fl oz) of the hot stock and add to the pan. Cook until the stock has been absorbed then add another 150 ml (5 fl oz). Continue cooking, adding more hot stock as it becomes absorbed, until all the stock has been used. This will take about 25 minutes, by which time the rice should be moist and tender but not mushy.
4. Take off the heat and using a fork lightly stir in the remaining butter and 50 g (2 oz) of Parmesan cheese, salt and plenty of pepper. Cover the pan and leave to stand for 3 minutes.
5. Serve hot, accompanied by the remaining Parmesan cheese.

SPINACH AND CHEESE LASAGNE

175g (6oz) wholewheat lasagne (about 10 sheets)

salt

paprika, to garnish

Filling:

2 × 225g (8oz) packets frozen spinach

freshly ground black pepper

1/4 teaspoon grated nutmeg

25g (1oz) pecan nuts, shelled and chopped.

Sauce:

40g (1 1/2oz) butter

40g (1 1/2oz) plain flour

600ml (1 pint) milk

200 (7oz) mature Cheddar cheese, grated

freshly ground black pepper

1/2 teaspoon made English mustard

Preparation time: *20 minutes*
Cooking time: *20-30 minutes*
Oven: *200°C, 400°F, Gas Mark 6*

The three parts of this straightforward recipe can be prepared more or less simultaneously. It is a simple matter then to put them in layers in the dish and brown them in the oven, and you have a good satisfying meal.

1. Cook the lasagne in boiling salted water for about 15 minutes (see hint box) until tender.

2. Meanwhile cook the spinach. Put the frozen spinach in a pan over a gentle heat, breaking the spinach up as it thaws. Simmer for about 2 minutes then increase the heat so that any liquid evaporates. Season with salt, pepper and nutmeg and stir in the nuts.

3. While the spinach is cooking make the sauce. Melt the butter, add the flour and cook for 3 minutes, stirring. Pour in the milk and bring to the boil stirring all the time until the sauce thickens and then simmer for 3 minutes. Add all but 25g (1oz) of the cheese and season with salt, pepper and mustard.

4. To assemble the dish, pour half the sauce into a shallow overproof serving dish and lay half the pasta sheets on top. Spoon the spinach over this and cover with the remaining pasta. Pour the rest of the sauce evenly over the top and sprinkle with the reserved cheese.

5. Bake near the top of the oven for 20-30 minutes until piping hot and brown on top.

6. Sprinkle with paprika and serve immediately.

COOKING LASAGNE SHEETS

A roasting tin is the best thing to use for cooking lasagne as it gives the pasta sheets plenty of room. When cooked, lift each sheet from the water separately with a fish slice and place in a pan or bowl of warm water. Keep the lasagne sheets in the warm water until needed but no longer than necessary, as they can absorb too much water. This will prevent the sheets from sticking together while the dish is assembled.

CALZONE

Serves 6

Yeast dough:

225g (8oz) strong plain wholemeal flour

225g (8oz) strong plain white flour

1 teaspoon salt

1 teaspoon caster sugar

1 sachet Easy Bake yeast

1 egg, lightly beaten

3 tablespoons vegetable oil

300ml (10fl oz) tepid milk

Filling:

1 tablespoon vegetable oil

3 medium onions, 225g (8oz), peeled and chopped

1 × 400g (14oz) can tomatoes

1 tablespoon tomato purée

2 teaspoons caster sugar

1 tablespoon fresh marjoram or 1 teaspoon dried marjoram

1/4 teaspoon cayenne pepper

freshly ground black pepper

175g (6oz) flat field mushrooms, chopped

175g (6oz) green pepper, seeded and chopped

225g (8oz) Mozzarella cheese, sliced

To finish:

beaten egg, for brushing

1 tablespoon sesame seeds

Preparation time: *45 minutes, plus rising*
Cooking time: *50-60 minutes*
Oven: *200°C, 400°F, Gas Mark 6;*
Then: *180°C, 350°F, Gas Mark 4*

1. First make the bread dough. Put the flours, salt, sugar and yeast into a large bowl. Make a well in the centre and add the egg, oil and milk.

2. Mix to a fairly firm consistency then turn on to a lightly floured surface and knead for about 5 minutes until the dough is smooth and elastic.

FROM THE LEFT Spinach and cheese lasagne; Calzone

3. Replace in the bowl, cover with a damp cloth and leave in a warm place for 1½ hours to rise. When the dough has doubled in size it is ready to use.

4. Meanwhile prepare the filling. Heat the oil in a pan and fry the onions gently for about 10 minutes until golden brown.

5. Add the tomatoes with their juice, tomato purée, sugar, marjoram, cayenne, salt and pepper. Break up the tomatoes a little with a wooden spoon. Cook over a steady heat, stirring occasionally for 10 minutes. Set aside to cool.

6. Turn the dough on to a lightly floured surface, knead for a moment or two and roll out to a rectangle measuring 50 × 25 cm (20 × 10 inches). Lay half the rectangle on a large greased baking sheet. This avoids moving the calzone once it has been assembled.

7. Spread half the tomato mixture over the dough on the sheet square to within 2.5 cm (1 inch) of the edges. Cover with the chopped mushrooms, then the peppers. Lay the slices of cheese side by side on top and cover with the remaining tomato mixture.

8. Brush the edges of the dough with beaten egg. Fold the dough over to cover the filling, making a fat square shape, and press the edges tightly together to seal. Brush all over with egg and sprinkle with sesame seeds.

9. Bake near the centre of the oven for 20 minutes then reduce the oven temperature and cook for a further 20-30 minutes. Cover the top with baking foil if necessary to prevent it browning too much.

10. Serve cut into thick slices, with a green salad.

COURGETTE AND WATERCRESS FLAN

Pastry:

175g (6oz) plain wholemeal flour	2 bunches watercress, stalks removed
salt	2 eggs
75g (3oz) hard vegetable margarine	150ml (5fl oz) soured cream
3 tablespoons water	5 tablespoons milk
1 tablespoon vegetable oil	freshly ground black pepper
Filling:	pinch of nutmeg
1 tablespoon vegetable oil	
3 small courgettes, about 100g (4oz), sliced	

Preparation time: *35 minutes*
Cooking time: *35 minutes*
Oven: *200°C, 400°F, Gas Mark 6*

A delicately flavoured flan which is perfect served hot with brown rice (see hint box), but equally good cold, accompanied by a tomato salad.

1. Make the pastry. Put the flour and ¼ teaspoon salt in a bowl and rub in the margarine until the mixture resembles fine breadcrumbs.

2. Using a round-bladed knife, mix to a firm dough with the water and oil. The oil will help to keep the pastry moist and light.

3. Roll out on a floured surface and use to line a 20cm (8 inch) fluted flan ring. Place the flan on a baking sheet and bake for 15 minutes to set the pastry without browning.

4. Meanwhile prepare the filling. Heat the oil in a pan and fry the courgettes quickly on both sides until brown. Drain on paper towels. Fry the watercress for 30 seconds until soft, then chop coarsely. Distribute the courgettes and watercress evenly over the base of the flan.

5. Put the eggs, soured cream, milk, salt, pepper and nutmeg into a bowl and whisk together.

6. Pull the centre shelf of the oven out slightly and place the flan case on it, then pour the egg and cream mixture over the courgettes and slide the shelf gently into place. This avoids spilling the liquid on the way to the oven.

7. Bake for 25 minutes until the flan is set and lightly browned. Ⓐ

Ⓐ The flan can be made up to 24 hours in advance and kept covered in the refrigerator. Warm through gently before serving.

COOKED BROWN RICE

275g (10oz) long-grain brown rice
1 teaspoon vegetable oil
1 teaspoon salt
750ml (1¼ pints) boiling water

PREPARATION TIME:
35 minutes

The nutty taste of brown rice goes well with everything. Cooked rice will keep well for 2 days, covered, in the refrigerator, and it's handy to have ready as the basis for a quick meal.

1. Put the rice, oil and salt into a medium-sized pan which has a tight-fitting lid.

2. Pour in the boiling water, bring back to the boil, give the rice a stir and put the lid on.

3. Turn the heat down and leave to simmer very gently for 35 minutes. The rice should now be cooked, though still with a 'bite' to it, and all the water will have been absorbed.

4. Stir briefly with a fork and serve.

5. If the rice is to be kept in the refrigerator, leave it to become quite cold before covering.

WINTER STEW WITH DUMPLINGS

Preparation time: *30 minutes*
Cooking time: *1½ hours*
Oven: *200°C, 400°F, Gas Mark 6*

2-3 tablespoons vegetable oil

1 large onion, peeled and chopped

3 carrots, about 175g (6oz), sliced

1 turnip, 175g (6oz), peeled and cut into 1 cm (½inch) cubes

1-2 parsnips, 175g (6oz), peeled and cut into short lengths

2 leeks, about 225g (8oz), halved, washed and sliced

3 potatoes, 450g (1lb), peeled and cut into 4cm (1½ inch) chunks

1 tablespoon plain white flour

1.2 litres (2 pints) hot vegetable stock

1 tablespoon tomato purée

¼ teaspoon celery seeds

salt

freshly ground black pepper

1 tablespoon chopped fresh parsley, to garnish

Dumplings:

175g (6oz) wholemeal self-raising flour

25g (1oz) hard vegetable margarine

1 teaspoon mixed dried herbs or 1 tablespoon mixed chopped fresh herbs

1 tablespoon vegetable oil

8 tablespoons water

A rich tasty vegetable casserole topped with herb dumplings. Each vegetable is browned in oil before being added to the casserole. This takes a little time but gives the finished dish a wonderful flavour. Serve with Lemon cabbage with poppyseeds (page 50) and crusty wholemeal bread to soak up the gravy.

1. Heat a little of the oil in a pan and fry the onion quickly until golden brown. Transfer to a large deep ovenproof casserole.

2. Adding a little more oil each time, brown each vegetable fairly quickly then transfer to the casserole.

3. When all the vegetables have been browned add a little more oil, stir in the flour, and cook over a steady heat stirring all the time until the flour is browned. Pour in the hot stock and bring to the boil stirring continuously until the stock has thickened slightly.

4. Add the tomato purée, celery seeds, salt and plenty of black pepper, then pour over the vegetables.

5. Put a lid on the casserole and leave to cook in the oven for 50 minutes. Ⓐ

6. Meanwhile make the dumplings. Put the flour into a bowl and rub in the margarine until the mixture resembles fine breadcrumbs. Then add the herbs and season with salt and pepper.

7. Mix to a very soft dough with the oil and water. Turn on to a floured surface and divide into 8 pieces. Shape each one lightly into a ball.

8. When the hotpot has cooked for 50 minutes remove the lid and add the dumplings. Replace the lid and put back into the oven for a further 20-30 minutes. The dumplings will rise to the top and swell to double their size.

10. Remove from the oven, sprinkle with parsley and serve immediately.

Ⓐ The hotpot can be prepared up to 24 hours in advance and kept covered. Reheat for about 30 minutes before adding the dumplings.

FROM THE LEFT Courgette and watercress flan; Winter stew with dumplings

FELAFEL IN PITTA POCKETS

Makes about 20

2 × 400g (14oz) cans chick peas

1 medium onion, peeled and grated

1 clove garlic, peeled and crushed (optional)

1 teaspoon ground cumin

1 teaspoon ground coriander

1/4 teaspoon ground chilli

1/2 teaspoon caraway seeds

salt

freshly ground black pepper

3 tablespoons chopped fresh parsley

1 egg, beaten

75g (3oz) wholemeal flour

vegetable oil, for shallow frying

To serve:

4 wholemeal pitta breads

1/2 cucumber, diced

4 small firm tomatoes, quartered

1 bunch watercress

crisp lettuce leaves

Preparation time: *20 minutes*
Cooking time: *20 minutes*
Oven: *110°C, 225°F, Gas Mark 1/4*

These little spiced fritters are a Middle Eastern speciality. They make an informal meal tucked inside pitta bread with salad and served with a side dish of Quick coleslaw (see hint box), but are also good as a starter served with Yogurt and watercress dressing (page 29) or mayonnaise. The use of canned chick peas for this recipe shortens the preparation time considerably.

1. Drain the chick peas and mash to a paste on a large plate a few at a time, using a fork or potato masher. (This can be done in a food processor if preferred.)

2. Put into a bowl with the onion, garlic, cumin, coriander, chilli, caraway seeds, salt and pepper. Mix to a firm paste then stir in the chopped parsley.

3. Form the mixture into small balls then pat them into small flat cakes about 4cm (1½ inches) across. Ⓐ Dip into beaten egg then into flour.

4. Shallow fry in oil in batches for about 5 minutes until crisp and brown. Drain on kitchen paper and keep hot in the oven while frying the rest. Put the pitta bread in the oven to warm before frying the last batch.

5. Split the pitta breads along one side with a sharp knife and fill the pocket with a mixture of cucumber, tomato, watercress, lettuce leaves and felafels. Serve immediately.

Ⓐ The uncooked felafel can be prepared up to 8 hours in advance and kept tightly covered with clingfilm to prevent the flavours permeating the other foods in the refrigerator.

QUICK COLESLAW

Make a quick, delicious coleslaw by combining ½ small white cabbage, finely shredded, with 2 large carrots, scrubbed and coarsely grated, 1 small onion, peeled and grated, salt, freshly ground black pepper and 150ml (5fl oz) soured cream.

POPOVERS WITH ONION AND TOMATO SAUCE

Makes 24 popovers

Onion and tomato Sauce:

1 tablespoon vegetable oil

1 large onion, peeled and thinly sliced

450 g (1 lb) ripe tomatoes, skinned and chopped

1 teaspoon soy sauce

2 teaspoons tomato purée

salt

freshly ground black pepper

Batter:

50 g (2 oz) plain wholemeal flour

50 g (2 oz) plain white flour

pinch of cayenne pepper

1 teaspoon mixed dried herbs

2 eggs, beaten

1 tablespoon vegetable oil, plus extra for greasing

150 ml (5 fl oz) milk

150 ml (5 fl oz) water

Preparation time: *25 minutes*
Cooking time: *25 minutes*
Oven: *220°C, 425°F, Gas Mark 7*

Serve the popovers piping hot from the oven with this thick piquant sauce. A quick, tasty and simple supper dish.

1. Heat the oil in a pan and fry the onion for 10 minutes until brown. Add the tomatoes, soy sauce, tomato purée, salt and plenty of pepper. Bring to simmering point, stirring, then cover the pan and cook gently for 10 minutes. Ⓐ Ⓕ

2. While the sauce is cooking make the batter. Put the flours, 1/2 teaspoon salt, pepper, cayenne and herbs into a bowl. Add the eggs, oil and half the milk and mix to a smooth paste. Gradually whisk in the remaining milk and the water. Pour the batter into a jug. Ⓐ

3. Generously oil 2 trays of 12 tart tins and put them in the preheated oven until smoking hot.

4. Remove from the oven, pour the batter into the tins, almost filling them, and bake for about 12 minutes until puffed up and golden brown.

5. Serve immediately with the hot sauce.

Ⓐ The sauce can be prepared up to 24 hours in advance and kept tightly covered with clingfilm in the refrigerator. Reheat when the popovers are ready to come out of the oven. The batter can be made up to 8 hours in advance and kept covered in the refrigerator.

Ⓕ The sauce can be frozen for up to 1 month. Thaw in a saucepan and reheat from frozen.

TWO-BEAN VEGETABLE GOULASH

100 g (4 oz) black beans, soaked overnight

100 g (4 oz) cannellini beans, soaked overnight

1 tablespoon vegetable oil

100 g (4 oz) very small onions or shallots, peeled but left whole

4 sticks of celery, scrubbed and sliced into chunks

4 small courgettes, cut into 2.5 cm (1 inch) chunks

3 small carrots, scrubbed and cut lengthways into chunks

1 × 400 g (14 oz) can tomatoes

300 ml (1/2 pint) vegetable stock

1 tablespoon paprika

1/2 teaspoon caraway seeds

salt

freshly ground black pepper

1 tablespoon cornflour

2 tablespoons water

150 ml (5 fl oz) soured cream, to serve (optional)

Preparation time: *30 minutes, plus overnight soaking*
Cooking time: *1 hour 20 minutes*

Black beans and cannellini beans have been chosen for this dish because they both take the same time to cook. If either is hard to find use haricot beans instead, but they will need longer to cook, about 1 1/2 hours. Warm granary rolls make a good accompaniment.

1. Drain the beans and rinse them under cold running water. Put them in two separate pans, cover with water and bring to the boil. Boil fast for 10 minutes then lower the heat, half cover the pans and simmer for about 1 hour until tender. Drain, rinse and set aside.

2. Heat the oil in a large pan with a lid and fry the onions, celery, courgettes and carrots quickly over a high heat until lightly browned.

3. Pour in the tomatoes with their juice and the stock. Stir in the paprika, caraway seeds, salt and pepper. Cover the pan and simmer for 20 minutes until the vegetables are tender.

4. Stir both lots of beans into the vegetables. Blend the cornflour with the water and add to the pan.

5. Bring to the boil stirring gently until the sauce thickens a little. Cover the pan and simmer again for about 10 minutes. Ⓐ

6. Spoon the goulash into a warm dish and serve with soured cream if liked.

Ⓐ The goulash can be prepared up to 24 hours in advance and kept tightly covered in the refrigerator. Reheat gently in a large pan for about 15 minutes.

FROM THE LEFT Felafel in pitta pockets shown with Quick coleslaw; Popovers with onion and tomato sauce; Two-bean vegetable goulash

PASTA WITH RICH TOMATO SAUCE

Serves 3-4
25 g (1 oz) butter
1 large onion, peeled and sliced
1 clove garlic, peeled and crushed (optional)
750 g (1 ½ lb) ripe tomatoes, skinned and chopped (see hint box)
1 tablespoon tomato purée
2 teaspoons caster or granulated sugar
2 tablespoons fresh marjoram or 2 teaspoons dried oregano
150 ml (5 fl oz) vegetable stock, or half stock and half red wine
salt
freshly ground black pepper

250 g (9 oz) wholewheat pasta shells or wholewheat spaghetti
Crunchy dressing (optional):
10 g (¼ oz) butter
25 g (1 oz) sunflower seeds
25 g (1 oz) wholewheat breadcrumbs

Preparation time: *25 minutes*
Cooking time: *30 minutes*

A good recipe for using over-ripe tomatoes.
1. Melt the butter in a pan and fry the onion and garlic for about 7 minutes until cooked but not brown.
2. Add the tomatoes, tomato purée, sugar, marjoram, stock (or stock and wine) salt and pepper. Half cover the pan and simmer gently for 25 minutes.
3. Remove the lid and cook a little faster for 2-3 minutes to reduce the sauce. It should have a thick, rich consistency. Keep hot. Ⓐ Ⓕ
4. Meanwhile cook the pasta. Bring a large pan of salted water to the boil, add the pasta and cook for about 15 minutes until just soft.
5. While the pasta is cooking prepare the dressing. Heat the butter in a frying pan, add the sunflower seeds and brown a little, stirring and shaking the pan (be careful as they will jump about in the heat) then stir in the breadcrumbs. When both are brown, spoon on to a plate and set aside.
6. Drain the pasta throughly, turn into a warm serving dish, spoon the hot sauce over, and top with the crunchy dressing. Serve immediately.
Ⓐ The sauce can be prepared up to 24 hours in advance and kept tightly covered.
Ⓕ The sauce can be frozen in a plastic container for up to 1 month and reheated gently from frozen.

SKINNING TOMATOES

Have ready a small pan of boiling water. Put the tomatoes into the water 2 at a time, leave for 6-10 seconds then lift out with a slotted spoon and leave to cool. With the tip of a sharp knife make a small nick in the top of each tomato and then peel off the skins. They should come off easily but if the tomatoes are slightly under-ripe they may need a few seconds longer in the boiling water before the skins can be removed.

FROM THE LEFT Pasta with rich tomato sauce; Bean and cabbage hotpot

BEAN AND CABBAGE HOTPOT

175g (6oz) aduki beans, soaked overnight in cold water	salt
	900ml (1½pints) hot vegetable stock
1 tablespoon vegetable oil	Topping:
3 medium onions, peeled and chopped	750g (1½lb) potatoes, cooked whole in their skins, then sliced
175g (6oz) carrots, scrubbed and sliced into rings	
350g (12oz) hard white cabbage, shredded	15g (½oz) butter, melted
½ teaspoon celery seed	paprika, to garnish
freshly ground black pepper	

Preparation time: *30 minutes, plus soaking overnight*
Cooking time: *1 hour 45 minutes*
Oven: *220°C, 425°F, Gas Mark 7*

Dark red aduki beans are easy to find in health-food shops. They have a nutty flavour which blends particularly well with the cabbage in this meal-in-a-pot recipe.

1. Drain the beans and then rinse under cold running water. Put them in a pan, cover with cold water and bring to the boil. Boil fast for 10 minutes then lower the heat. Half cover the pan and simmer for 35-45 minutes until tender. Drain, rinse and set aside.

2. Heat the oil in a large pan with a lid and cook the onions, carrots and cabbage, covered, for about 5 minutes.

3. Add the celery seed, plenty of black pepper and a little salt, then pour in the hot stock. Cover the pan and simmer gently for about 15 minutes then stir in the cooked beans.

4. Spoon the mixture into a large shallow casserole and arrange the slices of potatoes to cover the top. Ⓐ Brush with melted butter and bake near the top of the oven for about 30 minutes until the potatoes are browned and crisp. Sprinkle with paprika before serving.

Ⓐ The casserole can be prepared up to 8 hours in advance and kept covered. Increase cooking time to 50 minutes.

·S·I·D·E· D·I·S·H·E·S·

NEW POTATOES WITH FENNEL AND MINT

salt	freshly ground black pepper
1 kg (2 lb) tiny new potatoes	2 tablespoons chopped fresh mint, plus sprigs of mint to garnish
15 g (½ oz) butter	
1 small fennel bulb, trimmed and finely chopped	

Preparation time: *10 minutes*
Cooking time: *15-20 minutes*

Jersey or English new potatoes are the best for this dish, and combined with fennel and mint they are so good that they can even be enjoyed just on their own.
1. Bring a pan of salted water to the boil, and add the potatoes. Simmer for about 15 minutes until tender then drain.
2. Put the butter into the warm pan and heat gently. Add the fennel and fry for about 5 minutes until just beginning to brown then season well with pepper.
3. Tip the cooked potatoes into the pan, add the mint and toss the potatoes so that they are coated with butter, mint and fennel.
4. Serve hot, garnished with sprigs of mint.

OKRA AND MUSHROOMS WITH SUNFLOWER SEEDS

2 teaspoons vegetable oil	25 g (1 oz) butter
2 tablespoons sunflower seeds	100 g (4 oz) white button mushrooms, halved
350 g (12 oz) okra, washed, topped and tailed	salt
	freshly ground black pepper

Preparation time: *15 minutes*
Cooking time: *15-20 minutes*

Okra, sometimes called ladies' fingers, is available in most large stores as well as in oriental grocers.

1. Heat the oil in a small pan and cook the sunflower seeds for a minute or two until brown. Drain on kitchen paper and set aside.
2. It is best to cook the okra whole, but if any are too large cut them in half lengthways.
3. Melt the butter in a frying pan or wok and stir-fry the okra quickly for 3-4 minutes.
4. Add the mushrooms and cook for a further 3-4 minutes.
5. Sprinkle with salt and pepper, cover the pan and leave to cook for about 10 minutes, by which time the mushrooms should be soft and the okra crisply tender.
6. Remove the lid and cook quickly for a minute or two to reduce the liquid in the pan.
7. Spoon into a warm dish and sprinkle with the sunflower seeds.

SUMMER VEGETABLES WITH YOGURT AND MINT

225 g (8 oz) broad beans (weighed without pods)	150 ml (5 fl oz) plain unsweetened yogurt
salt	freshly ground black pepper
225 g (8 oz) runner beans, strings removed and sliced	1 tablespoon chopped fresh mint
225 g (8 oz) peas (weighed without pods)	

Preparation time: *25 minutes*
Cooking time: *15 minutes*

This can be made with frozen vegetables, cooking them for slightly less time than indicated on the packs.
1. Cook the broad beans for 8 minutes in a little boiling salted water then drain.
2. Cook the runner beans and peas together for 5 minutes and drain.
3. Heat the yogurt gently in one of the vegetable pans, add the vegetables and toss round to coat thoroughly.
4. Gently stir in black pepper and the mint and serve.

FROM THE TOP Okra and mushrooms with sunflower seeds; New potatoes with fennel and mint; Summer vegetables with yogurt and mint

LEMON CABBAGE WITH POPPY SEEDS

150 ml (5 fl oz) water	1 ½ teaspoons poppy seeds
½ teaspoon salt	freshly ground black pepper
350 g (12 oz) hard white cabbage, shredded	2-3 tablespoons soured cream, to serve (optional)
350 g (12 oz) spring greens or green cabbage, shredded	
25 g (1 oz) butter, cut into small pieces	
grated rind of 1 lemon	

Preparation time: 5 minutes
Cooking time: 10 minutes

The contrast provided by the green and white cabbage gives a particularly attractive appearance to this simple vegetable dish. It can be served with almost any main meal and is also delicious on its own with Hot mustard rolls (see hint box).

1. Put the water into a large pan, add the salt and bring to the boil. Add both green and white cabbage, cover and simmer steadily for 7-10 minutes. The cabbage should be crisply tender and most of the water absorbed.
2. Take the lid off the pan and boil quickly to reduce any remaining liquid.
3. Add the pieces of butter, lemon rind, poppy seeds and lots of black pepper. Stir briefly until the butter is melted and the cabbage well coated.
4. Spoon the hot cabbage into a warm dish and serve with soured cream spooned over the top if liked.

HOT MUSTARD ROLLS

These are best made with long, crusty rolls. Blend English, French or wholegrain mustard with freshly ground black pepper and butter, allowing 1 teaspoon of mustard to each 25 g (1 oz) of butter. Make 3 diagonal cuts almost through to the base of the rolls and spread the mustard butter on both sides of the cuts. Wrap the rolls individually in baking foil and put into a moderately hot oven (200°C, 400°F, Gas Mark 6) for 15 minutes until hot and crisp.

BEAN AND BEANSPROUT STIR-FRY

15 g (½ oz) butter	275 g (10 oz) beansprouts
1 tablespoon olive oil	salt
275 g (10 oz) French beans, or frozen whole green beans	freshly ground black pepper
	2 teaspoons paprika

Preparation time: 5 minutes
Cooking time: about 10 minutes

An interesting and quickly prepared vegetable side dish. If fresh beans are used, blanch them for 1 minute in boiling water then drain before stir-frying.

1. Heat the butter and oil in a wok or large frying pan until foamy then add the beans and stir-fry gently for about 4 minutes.
2. Push them to the sides of the wok, turn the heat up a little and add the beansprouts. Stir-fry for about 2 minutes.
3. Now mix the beans and beansprouts together adding a little salt, plenty of black pepper and the paprika. Stir-fry for 1 minute more, then turn into a warm serving dish and serve. Alternatively, serve straight from the wok.

CELERIAC STICKS WITH MUSTARD

750 g (1½ lb) celeriac	To garnish:
salt	lemon slices
1 tablespoon lemon juice	coriander leaves or parsley
Dressing:	sprigs
150 ml (5 fl oz) double or	
whipping cream or plain	
unsweetened yogurt	
freshly ground black pepper	
1 tablespoon wholegrain	
mustard	

Preparation time: *10 minutes*
Cooking time: *15-20 minutes*

FROM THE LEFT Bean and beansprout stir-fry; Celeriac sticks with mustard; Lemon cabbage with poppyseeds

Celeriac looks rather like a knobbly swede. As the name implies it tastes rather like celery, but it has a turnip-like texture. Cream and mustard turn it into a very special vegetable. This can be served as a starter if preferred.

1. Peel the celeriac and cut first into thick slices then into chips about 1 cm × 7.5 cm (½ inch × 3 inches).

2. Put the chips into a pan with a pinch of salt and the lemon juice and cover with water. Bring to the boil, cover the pan and simmer for 15-20 minutes until the celeriac is tender but still firm. Drain and keep warm in a serving dish.

3. Pour the cream or yogurt into the rinsed-out pan and stir in the salt, pepper and mustard. Heat very gently until hot, *but do not let it boil.*

4. Pour the cream and mustard dressing over the celeriac and garnish with lemon slices and the coriander leaves or parsley. Serve immediately.

CAULIFLOWER WITH PEANUT SAUCE

1 medium cauliflower, about 500g (1¼lb)	½ teaspoon yeast extract
salt	freshly ground black pepper
2 tablespoons chopped salted peanuts, to garnish	
Sauce:	
15g (½oz) butter	
15g (½oz) plain flour	
150ml (¼pint) milk	
150ml (¼pint) vegetable stock	
4 tablespoons crunchy peanut butter	

Preparation time: *25 minutes*
Cooking time: *15 minutes*

A side dish that is almost a meal in itself. Serve with brown rice and grilled tomatoes for a quick supper.
1. Cut the cauliflower into florets, leaving some of the contrasting green leaves on. Cook the cauliflower in boiling salted water for about 6-8 minutes; it should still be slightly crisp. Drain and keep warm in a serving dish.
2. While the cauliflower is cooking make the sauce. Melt the butter in a small pan, add the flour and cook for 3 minutes, stirring all the time.
3. Pour in the milk and vegetable stock and bring to the boil, still stirring. Simmer for 2-3 minutes then stir in the peanut butter, a spoonful at a time. The peanut butter will thicken the sauce.
4. Add the yeast extract, a little salt if necessary (there is probably enough in the peanut butter) and black pepper.
5. Pour the sauce over the cauliflower and sprinkle with the chopped peanuts. Serve hot.

KARTOSHKI

Serves 2-3

15g (½oz) butter	freshly ground black pepper
1 tablespoon oil	2 spring onions, chopped
450g (1 lb) small potatoes, unpeeled and fairly thickly sliced	
salt	

Preparation time: *5 minutes*
Cooking time: *20 minutes*

This is an economical way of cooking potatoes, and produces an almost roast taste without using the oven. A traditional Russian recipe.
1. Use the largest frying pan you have and heat the butter and oil until sizzling.
2. Add the potatoes and stir until all the slices are coated and glistening. Keep the heat high and fry them quickly until golden brown but not cooked.
3. Turn the slices and sprinkle generously with salt and black pepper. Cover the frying pan, lower the heat and continue to fry/steam the slices for about 20 minutes until tender, shaking the pan occasionally to prevent them sticking.
4. Take the lid off the pan and turn up the heat again for a minute or two.
5. Serve immediately sprinkled with the spring onion.

BRAISED ONIONS IN CIDER AND SAGE

2 large Spanish onions, about 450g (1 lb)	1 teaspoon cornflour
1 tablespoon vegetable oil	1 tablespoon water
300ml (½pint) dry cider	
salt	
freshly ground black pepper	
2 teaspoons chopped fresh sage or ½ teaspoon dried sage	

Preparation time: *15 minutes*
Cooking time: *1 hour*
Oven: *180°C, 350°F, Gas Mark 4*

A delicious and attractive way to serve the mild-flavoured Spanish onions — braised in a golden sage and cider flavoured sauce.
1. Remove the papery skins from the onions and cut each into 4. Trim the bases very lightly so that the quarters stay intact during cooking.
2. Heat the oil in a frying pan and quickly fry the onion quarters on all sides until golden brown. Place them in a small shallow casserole, cut-side up.
3. Pour the cider into the pan with the salt, pepper and sage. Bring to the boil then pour over the onions.
4. Cover the casserole and bake for 40 minutes.
5. Remove from the oven, blend the cornflour with the water and stir into the liquor surrounding the onions. Cover again and replace in the oven for a further 20 minutes by which time the onions will be tender and the sauce slightly thickened.
6. Serve hot.

CLOCKWISE FROM THE TOP Cauliflower with peanut sauce; Kartoshki; Braised onions in cider and sage

◆ 53 ◆

FRUIT AND VEGETABLE KEBABS

8 button onions, peeled and left whole	Marinade:
1 small green pepper, seeded and cut into 8 pieces	6 tablespoons vegetable oil
	1 tablespoon lemon juice
1 small red pepper, seeded and cut into 8 pieces	1 teaspoon grated orange rind
16 button mushrooms, wiped	1 tablespoon finely chopped walnuts
2 large bananas, peeled and cut into 8 chunks	salt
1 × 350g (12oz) can pineapple cubes, drained	freshly ground black pepper

Preparation time: *20 minutes*
Cooking time: *8 minutes*

These quickly cooked and colourful kebabs provide an interesting combination of tastes. Cooked brown rice (page 42) or Risotto Milanese (page 39) would be just right to serve with them.
1. Blanch the onions and peppers in boiling water for 3 minutes so that they cook in the same time as the other ingredients. Drain and pat dry with kitchen paper.
2. Thread all the ingredients on to 8 kebab skewers. Lay the kebabs in a shallow dish while you make the marinade.
3. Stir the oil, lemon juice, orange rind, walnuts, salt and pepper together in a small bowl.
4. Spoon the marinade over the kebabs. Cover and leave for about 1 hour, basting with the marinade occasionally.
5. Lay the kebabs on a foil-lined baking sheet and place under a medium grill. Grill for 8-10 minutes for until evenly browned, turning them during cooking and brushing with the marinade. Serve hot.

MIXED VEGETABLE STIR-FRY

1 small cauliflower, about 350g (12oz)	2 sticks of celery
	1 tablespoon vegetable oil
2 medium carrots, about 100g (4oz)	15g (1/2oz) butter
	2 tablespoons pumpkin seeds
2 courgettes, about 175g (6oz)	salt
	freshly ground black pepper

Preparation time: *20 minutes*
Cooking time: *8-10 minutes*

This is one of the best ways to cook vegetables. The colours stay bright and the quick cooking without water retains all

FROM THE LEFT Fruit and vegetable kebabs; Curried sweetcorn and potato fritters shown with Yogurt and watercress dressing (recipe on page 29); Mixed vegetable stir-fry

the goodness. Use other combinations of vegetables if you prefer, but be sure to cut them all in tiny pieces to ensure they cook quickly and remain crisp.

1. Cut the cauliflower into very small florets.
2. Scrub the carrots and cut into thin strips about 3 mm × 4 cm (⅛ inch × 1½ inches).
3. Cut the courgettes into chunks then into strips like the carrots.
4. Trim the celery and cut it into 4 cm (1½ inch) lengths then into strips in the same way.
5. Heat the oil and butter together in a wok or large frying pan. Add the pumpkin seeds and fry for about 1 minute, taking care as they will jump about in the heat.
6. Add all the vegetables at once, sprinkle with salt and pepper and cook over a steady heat, shaking the pan and turning the vegetables lightly for about 8-10 minutes until crisply tender.
7. Serve immediately.

CURRIED SWEETCORN AND POTATO FRITTERS

Makes about 20
50 g (2 oz) plain wholemeal flour
½ teaspoon salt
freshly ground black pepper
1 egg, lightly beaten
4 tablespoons milk
1 teaspoon hot curry paste
450 g (1 lb) potatoes, unpeeled, washed and coarsely grated
1 medium onion, peeled and grated
1 × 200 g (7 oz) can sweetcorn, drained

4-6 tablespoons vegetable oil, for frying

Preparation time: *25 minutes*
Cooking time: *25 minutes*
Oven: *110°C, 250°F, Gas Mark ¼*

These crisp, spicy, hot fritters can be served as part of a meal or as a light supper dish with a bowl of Yogurt and watercress dressing (page 29). Use a milder curry paste if you prefer. Cook the mixture soon after making it, as it tends to discolour a little if left to stand.

1. Put the flour, salt, pepper, egg, milk and curry paste into a large bowl and mix to a smooth, thick batter.
2. Put the grated potato into a clean cloth and twist both ends towards the middle to squeeze out any surplus starchy liquid. This ensures the fritters will be crisp.
3. Pat the potato dry with kitchen paper and add to the batter with the onion and sweetcorn.
4. Heat 1 tablespoon of oil in a large frying pan and drop the mixture in 1 tablespoon at a time, gently nudging each fritter into a round flat shape with a fish slice. Cook about 4 fritters at a time.
5. Fry the fritters for 3-4 minutes on each side, then drain on kitchen paper and keep hot while frying the next batch. Alternatively, if time is short, fry the mixture all at once. Divide it between 2 frying pans and make 2 large fritters, increasing the cooking time by about 2 minutes for each side, and cutting the fritters in half to turn them easily.
6. Arrange the fritters on a warm dish and serve.

FROM THE LEFT Leek, potato and coriander bake; Pan-braised peppers with tomato; Button mushrooms with green peppercorns

LEEK, POTATO AND CORIANDER BAKE

450 g (1 lb) leeks, trimmed and washed	25 g (1 oz) butter
1 kg (2 lb) small potatoes, scrubbed and dried	1 teaspoon black peppercorns
1 tablespoon oil	2 teaspoons coriander seeds
	1 teaspoon sea salt

Preparation time. *15 minutes*
Cooking time: *1¼ hours*
Oven: *200°C, 400°F, Gas Mark 6*

Use a waxy type of potato like a Cyprus or Jersey for this dish. It should be cooked in a large shallow roasting tin to make sure the potatoes and leeks are spread in one layer and become nicely browned. Serve it by itself or as an accompaniment to almost any dish.
1. Slice the leeks into 2 cm (¾ inch) rings and cut the potatoes into 1 cm (½ inch) slices.
2. Put the oil and butter in a large shallow roasting tin and place in the oven until the butter is just melted.
3. Add the leeks and potatoes, turning them over several times to coat them with the oil and butter.
4. Crush the peppercorns with the coriander seeds. If you have no pestle and mortar, put the seeds and peppercorns between two double sheets of kitchen paper or grease-

proof paper and crush firmly with a rolling pin.

5. Put the crushed pepper and coriander in a small bowl, add the salt, sprinkle evenly over the potatoes and leeks and stir them through.

6. Cover the tin tightly with baking foil and place in the oven for 45 minutes. After this time remove the foil, turn the potatoes and leeks over and put back near the top of the oven for a further 30 minutes to become brown.

7. Serve hot.

PAN-BRAISED PEPPERS WITH TOMATO

1 tablespoon vegetable oil	½ teaspoon salt
2 medium onions, peeled and coarsely chopped	½ teaspoon ground chilli
3 large peppers, red, green and yellow, total weight about 450 g (1 lb), seeded and cut into strips	
450 g (1 lb) tomatoes, skinned and chopped	
1 teaspoon coriander seeds, crushed	
1 teaspoon black peppercorns, crushed	

Preparation time: *25 minutes*
Cooking time: *20 minutes*

A vegetable recipe full of flavour and colour. It is not essential to use different coloured peppers, but it does look attractive. This dish is wonderful hot and almost as good served cold with a salad selection.

1. Heat the oil in a large frying pan and fry the onions for about 5 minutes until golden.

2. Add the peppers and cook gently for 2-3 minutes, then stir in the tomatoes.

3. Crush the coriander seeds and peppercorns. Use a pestle and mortar if you have one; otherwise put the seeds and peppercorns between double sheets of kitchen paper and crush with a rolling pin.

4. Add the salt and chilli to the crushed seeds and sprinkle the mixture over the peppers and tomatoes.

5. Mix together lightly, cover the pan and cook gently for 20 minutes. Ⓐ Ⓕ

Ⓐ Can be prepared up to 24 hours in advance and kept covered in the refrigerator.

Ⓕ Can be frozen in a rigid plastic container for up to 1 month. Thaw at room temperature and reheat gently.

BUTTON MUSHROOMS WITH GREEN PEPPERCORNS

450 g (1 lb) small white button mushrooms	coriander leaves, or sprigs of parsley, to garnish
1 tablespoon olive oil	
4 tablespoons water	
salt	
4 slices brown bread	
2 tablespoons vegetable oil	
25 g (1 oz) butter	
3 teaspoons green peppercorns, lightly crushed	
2 tablespoons double or whipping cream	

Preparation time: *10 minutes*
Cooking time: *15 minutes*

A simple but unusual way to serve button mushrooms which also makes a delicious starter. Green peppercorns are sold either in jars or small cans in most delicatessens or large stores. They are quite soft, and so can be crushed easily.

1. Wash the mushrooms and pat them dry on kitchen paper. If they are all small leave them whole, but halve any larger ones.

2. Heat the oil in a large frying pan and fry the mushrooms quickly for about 5 minutes until just beginning to brown.

3. Add the water and a little salt, cover the pan and simmer for about 10 minutes, by which time there will be a fair amount of liquid in the pan.

4. While the mushrooms are cooking, make the croûtons. Cut the crusts off the bread and cut the slices into 1 cm (½ inch) dice.

5. Heat the oil and butter in a frying pan until sizzling and add the croûtons. Fry quickly until golden brown then drain on kitchen paper.

6. Stir the peppercorns and cream into the mushrooms and reheat gently without boiling. Tip into a warm serving dish and scatter with the croûtons.

7. Garnish with the coriander leaves or parsley sprigs and serve immediately.

COLCANNON

225g (8oz) shredded white cabbage	25g (1oz) butter
salt	1 medium onion, peeled and chopped
500g (1¼lb) potatoes, cooked and mashed without milk or butter	freshly ground black pepper
	2 teaspoons poppy seeds

Preparation time: 15 minutes
Cooking time: 40 minutes
Oven: 200°C, 400°F, Gas Mark 6

This dish, which can be served with the Two-bean vegetable goulash (page 45), Rich tomato sauce (page 46) or just on its own, is an excellent way of using the insides of the potatoes left from the Fried potato jackets (page 16).
1. Cook the cabbage in a little boiling salted water for about 6 minutes until crisply tender. Drain and put into a bowl with the mashed potato.
2. Meanwhile melt half the butter in a small pan and gently fry the onion until golden. Stir into the cabbage and potato and add a little salt and plenty of black pepper.
3. Use the remaining 15g (½oz) butter to grease a 450g (1lb) loaf tin, and scatter the poppy seeds over the base and sides of the tin to coat.
4. Spoon the cabbage and potato mixture into the tin, smooth the top and cover with foil.
5. Bake for 40 minutes, then turn out on to a hot dish and serve immediately.

CORN ON THE COB WITH HERBS

4 corn cobs, husks and silky threads removed	freshly ground black pepper
50g (2oz) butter	2 teaspoons chopped mixed fresh herbs (parsley, thyme and chives)
salt	

Preparation time: 15 minutes
Cooking time: 25-30 minutes
Oven: 200°C, 400°F, Gas Mark 6

Use frozen corn-on-the-cob when fresh corn is out of season, but it will require 10 minutes boiling at step 1. It is important not to salt the cooking water for this vegetable as it tends to make it tough.
1. Bring a large pan of unsalted water to the boil, add the cobs, cook for 15 minutes and drain.
2. Blend together the butter, salt, pepper and herbs. Spread a little over each corn-cob and wrap each one in a piece of baking foil, crimping the edges securely together.
3. Place on a baking sheet in the oven for 20 minutes. Unwrap the foil parcels carefully and serve the corn on hot plates with the herb and butter juices poured over.

BABY PARSNIPS IN BREADCRUMBS

450g (1lb) very small parsnips, scrubbed if necessary	75g (3oz) fresh wholemeal breadcrumbs
salt	2 tablespoons freshly grated Parmesan cheese
1 tablespoon vegetable oil	1 tablespoon chopped fresh parsley, to garnish
freshly ground black pepper	

Preparation time: 15 minutes
Cooking time: 30-35 minutes
Oven: 220°C, 425°F, Gas Mark 7

If the parsnips are very tiny they look best cooked whole, otherwise cut them in half lengthways.
1. Cook the parsnips in boiling salted water for 7-10 minutes until just tender. Drain and return to the pan.
2. Toss them in the oil and plenty of black pepper. Mix the breadcrumbs, Parmesan cheese and ½ teaspoon salt, add to the pan and toss again.
3. Spoon the parsnips and any crumbs left in the pan into a lightly oiled ovenproof dish and bake near the top of the oven for 15-20 minutes until the breadcrumbs are crisp and lightly browned.
4. Sprinkle with chopped parsley and serve immediately.

BROAD BEANS WITH SESAME

450g (1lb) broad beans, prepared weight, fresh or frozen	1 tablespoon lemon juice
	freshly ground black pepper
2 tablespoons sesame seeds	
25g (1oz) butter	

Preparation time: 5 minutes for frozen beans, 15 minutes for fresh beans
Cooking time: 10-15 minutes

Sesame seeds add a special flavour of their own to a variety of foods, and seem to go particularly well with broad beans.
1. Cook the beans in boiling salted water until tender, 8-15 minutes depending on whether fresh or frozen.
2. While the beans are cooking toast the sesame seeds under a moderate grill to brown them evenly.
3. Drain the beans, and put the butter in the pan. Melt it quickly and when just beginning to brown add the lemon juice and pepper.
4. Tip the beans back into the pan and toss well in the butter.
5. Serve sprinkled with the sesame seeds.

CLOCKWISE FROM THE TOP Broad beans with sesame; Colcannon; Baby parsnips in breadcrumbs; Corn on the cob with herbs

S·A·L·A·D·S

GREEN AND GOLD SALAD

1 ripe avocado	25g (1 oz) grated Parmesan cheese, to garnish
1 tablespoon lemon juice	
8 slices cut from a French loaf	Dressing:
	6 tablespoons olive oil
vegetable oil, for shallow frying	1 tablespoon lemon juice
	1 clove garlic, peeled and crushed (optional)
1 small cos or Webb lettuce, torn into pieces	
	salt
4 hard-boiled eggs, shelled and quartered	freshly ground black pepper
	2-3 drops Tabasco sauce
1 bunch watercress, washed and trimmed into sprigs	

Preparation time: *25 minutes*

A colourful salad that also makes a complete meal just served with a bottle of wine.
1. Peel, stone and slice the avocado and sprinkle the slices with lemon juice to prevent them from discolouring.
2. Cut each slice of bread into 4 quarters and fry quickly for 1 minute until golden. Drain on kitchen paper and set aside.
3. Put the avocado in a large bowl with the lettuce and hard-boiled eggs then add the fried bread croûtons and watercress.
4. Make the dressing. In a small bowl whisk together the oil, lemon juice, garlic, salt, pepper and Tabasco until blended. Pour over the salad and toss lightly to coat thoroughly with the dressing.
5. Sprinkle with Parmesan cheese and serve.

CARROT AND APPLE SALAD

350g (12oz) carrots, coarsely grated	2 teaspoons vegetable oil
	2 tablespoons cashew nuts
3 Cox's Orange Pippins, unpeeled, cored and sliced	1 quantity Light French dressing (see Orange winter salad, page 65)
1 tablespoon lemon juice	
1 tablespoon sunflower seeds	lettuce leaves, to serve
3 tablespoons raisins	

Preparation time: *20 minutes*

This vitamin-rich salad should be prepared just before serving, so that it is crisp and fresh. It looks attractive served on a bed of lettuce.
1. Put the grated carrot into a large bowl. Sprinkle the apple slices with lemon juice to prevent them discolouring then add to the bowl.
2. Lightly mix in the sunflower seeds and raisins.
3. Heat the oil in a small pan and lightly brown the cashew nuts. Lift out and drain on kitchen paper then add to the bowl.
4. Spoon the French dressing over the salad and toss lightly. Serve on a bed of lettuce leaves.

HOT RED BEAN AND SWEETCORN SALAD

1 × 400g (14oz) can red kidney beans, drained	Dressing:
	6 tablespoons olive oil
1 × 200g (7oz) can sweetcorn, drained	1 tablespoon wine vinegar
	salt
4 sticks celery, trimmed, scrubbed and chopped	freshly ground black pepper
	½ teaspoon Tabasco sauce
1 Spanish onion, peeled and very thinly sliced into rings	½ teaspoon mustard powder
	2 green chillies, seeded and finely chopped (or to taste)
mustard and cress, to garnish	

Preparation time: *15 minutes*

An easy salad to serve for a winter lunch with granary bread and unsalted butter. Spinach soup (page 10) would make a good starter.
1. Put the beans, sweetcorn, celery and onion into a bowl.
2. In a smaller bowl mix together the oil, vinegar, salt, pepper, Tabasco, mustard and chillies.
3. Pour over the bean mixture and turn lightly to coat thoroughly with the dressing.
4. Spoon into a serving dish and leave covered for 1-2 hours to allow the flavours to mature. Ⓐ
5. Just before serving, garnish with the mustard and cress.
Ⓐ Can be left to marinate for up to 8 hours, tightly covered in clingfilm in the refrigerator.

FROM THE TOP Green and gold salad; Carrot and apple salad; Hot red bean and sweetcorn salad

MIXED SALAD CHOICE

Serves 6

a) 175 g (6 oz) grated carrot
   25 g (1 oz) raisins
b) 1 × 100 g (4 oz) can sweetcorn, drained
   50 g (2 oz) small button mushrooms, sliced
c) 175 g (6 oz) beansprouts
   1 small green pepper, seeded and finely sliced
d) 175 g (6 oz) iceberg lettuce, shredded
   100 g (4 oz) cucumber, unpeeled and diced
e) 4 sticks of celery, trimmed, scrubbed and chopped
   2 red apples, unpeeled, cored and diced
   1 tablespoon of lemon juice

f) 6 small firm tomatoes, sliced
   2 spring onions, trimmed, peeled and sliced
g) 6 hard-boiled eggs, shelled and quartered (optional)
   paprika, to sprinkle (optional)
h) 1 × 225 g (8 oz) carton cottage cheese
   50 g (2 oz) grapes, halved and seeded

To serve:
Piquant creamy dressing (right)
Lemon and mustard dressing (below)
Hot garlic bread (page 65)

Preparation time: 40 minutes

This colourful selection of salads takes time to assemble, but the inviting result is well worth the effort. It makes the perfect self-service lunch or evening snack.
1. Prepare the various salad combinations as indicated above and arrange them either separately on a large platter or on individual small dishes.
2. Make the two dressings and prepare the garlic bread.
3. Lay out the buffet and allow guests to choose their own combinations of salads and dressings.

LEMON AND MUSTARD DRESSING

175 ml (6 fl oz) olive oil
2 tablespoons lemon juice
grated rind of 1 lemon
1 teaspoon caster sugar
1 teaspoon salt
freshly ground black pepper

½ teaspoon English mustard powder

PREPARATION TIME: 5 minutes

1. Whisk all the ingredients together in a bowl.

PIQUANT CREAMY DRESSING

150 ml (5 fl oz) low-calorie mayonnaise
150 ml (5 fl oz) soured cream
12 stuffed olives, finely chopped
2 teaspoons grated onion
2 teaspoons tomato purée
salt
freshly ground black pepper
pinch of chilli powder

2 tablespoons chopped fresh parsley

PREPARATION TIME: 10 minutes

1. Mix the mayonnaise and soured cream together in a bowl, then stir in the olives, onion, tomato purée, salt, pepper and chilli.
2. Adjust seasoning then stir in the parsley.

PIQUANT POTATO SALAD

750 g (1½ lb) tiny new potatoes
salt
Dressing:
3 tablespoons olive oil
1 tablespoon white wine vinegar
freshly ground black pepper
½ teaspoon made English mustard

2 teaspoons capers, finely chopped
1 pickled gherkin, finely chopped
1 tablespoon chopped fresh parsley

Preparation time: 5 minutes
Cooking time: 15-20 minutes

If you cannot find really small potatoes, use slightly larger ones and cut them in half after cooking. This can be served as part of a salad selection or it makes a perfect accompaniment to warm Courgette and watercress flan (page 42).
1. Wash the potatoes and place in a pan of boiling salted water. Cook for 15-20 minutes until just tender. Drain and tip into a bowl.
2. While the potatoes are cooking prepare the dressing. Put the oil and vinegar into a small bowl and stir in the salt, pepper, mustard, capers and gherkins. Add the chopped parsley.
3. Pour the dressing over the hot potatoes and stir gently to coat them all thoroughly. Leave to cool, but do not chill. Ⓐ
4. Serve in a shallow dish at room temperature.
Ⓐ The salad can be prepared up to 8 hours in advance and kept covered in the refrigerator but remember to take it from the refrigerator 30 minutes before serving.

FROM THE LEFT Mixed salad choice shown with Lemon and mustard dressing, Piquant creamy dressing and Hot garlic bread (recipe page 65); Spinach, chicory and mushroom salad

BEANSPROUT, CELERY AND LANCASHIRE CHEESE SALAD

275g (10g) beansprouts	Dressing:
½ cucumber, about 225g (8oz), unpeeled and cut into strips 3mm × 5cm (⅛ × 2 inches)	6 tablespoons olive oil
	1 tablespoon white wine vinegar
4 sticks celery, scrubbed and cut into strips 3mm × 5cm (⅛ inch × 2 inches)	½ teaspoon made English mustard
	salt
1 bunch watercress washed and trimmed into sprigs, to garnish	freshly ground black pepper
	75g (3oz) Lancashire cheese, crumbled

Preparation time: *20 minutes*

A crisp, quickly made salad. Add the dressing just before serving to keep it all fresh.

1. Combine the beansprouts, cucumber and celery in a large bowl.
2. In a small bowl whisk together the oil, vinegar, mustard, salt and pepper, then add the crumbled cheese.
3. Pour over the salad and toss lightly with two forks so that it is thoroughly coated with dressing.
4. Tuck the sprigs of watercress here and there into the salad and serve.

SPINACH, CHICORY AND MUSHROOM SALAD

225g (8oz) fresh young spinach leaves	1 head chicory, separated into leaves
100g (4oz) small button mushrooms, sliced thinly	
1 quantity Light French dressing (see Orange winter salad, page 65)	

Preparation time: *10 minutes*

A simple, quickly prepared salad which makes a change from the lettuce-based green salads. Serve with a dish of quartered hard-boiled eggs and some warm French bread for an informal light lunch.

1. Remove the stems from the spinach leaves and wash them in several changes of water. Pat dry on kitchen paper and, using scissors, snip into narrow strips about 1cm (½ inch) wide.
2. Mix the mushrooms into the spinach. Pour the dressing over and toss the salad until throughly coated.
3. Place in a serving bowl, tuck leaves of chicory in here and there, and serve immediately.

TROPICAL SALAD

275 g (10 oz) long-grain
brown rice, cooked (page 42)
50 g (2 oz) dried coconut
flakes
½ cucumber, unpeeled and
cut into 1 cm (½ inch) cubes
1 small ripe pineapple,
peeled, cored and cut into
2.5 cm (1 inch) pieces
1 tablespoon olive oil
1 teaspoon lemon juice
salt
freshly ground black pepper
To garnish:
2 teaspoons olive oil

50 g (2 oz) whole blanched
almonds
pineapple leaves

Preparation time: *15 minutes, plus cooking time for rice*

An unusual and delicious salad. You will find coconut flakes or slices in many health food shops but unsweetened desiccated coconut can be used instead, and you can even use a 400 g (14 oz) can of pineapple if fresh fruit is not available.
1. Put the rice, coconut, cucumber and pineapple into a bowl.
2. Add the oil and lemon juice and a little salt and pepper, taste and adjust the seasoning if necessary, then spoon into a serving dish.
3. Heat the 2 teaspoons of oil in a small pan, put in the almonds and fry quickly until golden brown.
4. Scatter the almonds over the salad and garnish with the pineapple leaves.

FROM THE LEFT Tropical salad; Orange winter salad; Pasta, cucumber and radish salad

ORANGE WINTER SALAD

	Light French dressing:
4 large oranges	5 tablespoons olive oil
1 × 400g (14oz) can red kidney beans, drained	2 tablespoons lemon juice
275g (10oz) beansprouts	salt
4 sticks of celery, trimmed, scrubbed and thinly sliced	1/4 teaspoon sugar
	freshly ground black pepper
sprigs of watercress, to garnish	1/4 teaspoon made English mustard

Preparation time: *15 minutes*

Nutritionally this crisp colourful salad has everything. It's good in the winter too, when other salad ingredients are expensive.

1. Using a serrated knife cut the top and bottom from the oranges then remove all the skin and pith, leaving a ball of fruit. Cut into segments by cutting down on either side of each membrane, and put in a bowl with any juice that runs out while cutting.

2. Add the beans, beansprouts and celery and toss lightly together.

3. Now make the dressing. Put the oil, lemon juice, salt, sugar, pepper and mustard into a screw-top jar and shake vigorously until blended.

4. Just before serving the salad spoon the dressing over and garnish with watercress.

PASTA, CUCUMBER AND RADISH SALAD

100g (4oz) pasta shapes (shells, bows or spirals)	150ml (5fl oz) soured cream
	freshly ground black pepper
salt	1 cos lettuce, washed and dried
175g (6oz) radishes, trimmed, washed and sliced	
1/2 cucumber, about 225g (8oz), unpeeled and diced	2 spring onions, trimmed, peeled and finely chopped, to garnish

Preparation time: *25 minutes*

An easily prepared lunch-time salad. Serve with Hot garlic bread (see box hint) and dry white wine.

1. Put the pasta into a large pan of boiling salted water. Bring back to the boil and cook for about 10 minutes until 'al dente'. Rinse under cold running water and drain thoroughly.

2. Put the radishes and cucumber into a bowl and add the pasta.

3. Stir in the soured cream adding plenty of black pepper and a little salt. Turn the pasta, radishes and cucumber over in the cream to coat thoroughly.

4. Arrange the lettuce leaves on a serving dish and spoon the salad into them. Garnish with the chopped spring onions.

HOT GARLIC BREAD

150g (5oz) butter	**1.** Using a fork, mix together the butter, salt and garlic cloves.
1/4 teaspoon salt	
3 garlic cloves, peeled and crushed	**2.** Cut the loaves into 5cm (2 inch) thick slices. Spread the garlic butter on both sides of each slice and put the slices back together to reshape the loaves. Wrap in foil and bake for 10 minutes. Unwrap carefully and serve immediately.
2 wholemeal French loaves	
PREPARATION TIME: *15 minutes*	
COOKING TIME: *10 minutes*	
OVEN: *220°C, 425°F, Gas Mark 7*	

P·U·D·D·I·N·G·S

MELON AND RASPBERRIES IN SAUTERNES

1 small ripe Galia melon	½ bottle Sauternes, chilled
175g (6oz) fresh or thawed frozen raspberries	

Preparation time: *5 minutes, plus chilling*

The quickest and most elegant way of enjoying wine and fruit together. Arrange a few rose petals as a decoration round the stem of each glass.

1. Halve the melon and either scoop out small balls using a melon baller or cut the flesh into small cubes.
2. Divide the melon and raspberries equally between 4 glass dishes. Pour over any melon juice, cover and chill in the refrigerator for at least 2 hours.
3. Just before serving, pour the chilled Sauternes into each dish to almost cover the fruit. Serve immediately.

WINTER RHUBARB JELLY

450g (1 lb) pink forced rhubarb	150ml (5fl oz) fresh orange juice
2 tablespoons light soft brown sugar	4 tablespoons clear honey
4 tablespoons water	1 teaspoon agar agar (see page 8)
¼ teaspoon ground cinnamon	8 Honey oat biscuits, crumbled (optional)

Preparation time: *25 minutes, plus setting overnight*

Use tender forced rhubarb when available; summer garden rhubarb can be used, but will not supply the same delicate colour. Omit the crunchy topping if preferred.

1. Cut the rhubarb into 2.5cm (1 inch) lengths and put in a pan with the sugar, water and cinnamon.
2. Cover the pan and cook gently for about 10 minutes until the rhubarb has softened to a pulp.
3. Meanwhile put the orange juice, honey and agar agar into a small pan and bring to the boil.
4. Pour on to the rhubarb and stir well. Taste for sweetness and add extra honey if necessary.

5. Pour the mixture into a large glass dish and leave to refrigerate overnight.
6. Just before serving, sprinkle with crumbled biscuits if liked.

CRANACHAN WITH FRUIT KISSEL

Kissel:	2 tablespoons water
450g (1 lb) fresh or frozen soft fruits (choose 3-4 from raspberries, redcurrants, loganberries, strawberries, blackcurrants or blackberries)	Cranachan:
	150ml (5fl oz) double or whipping cream
50g (2oz) light soft brown sugar	150ml (5fl oz) single cream
	few drops vanilla essence
150ml (5fl oz) unsweetened orange juice	40g (1½oz) coarse oatmeal, toasted
2 teaspoons cornflour	1 tablespoon light soft brown sugar

Preparation time: *20 minutes, plus chilling*
Cooking time: *5 minutes*

An unforgettable combination of simple puddings which complement one another deliciously.

1. Make the kissel: pick over, wash and prepare the fruits. Frozen fruits need not be thawed. Place in a bowl.
2. Dissolve the sugar in the orange juice over a low heat. Mix the cornflour to a smooth paste with the water and add to the pan. Bring to the boil, stirring, until the sauce clears and thickens.
3. Pour over the fruit and stir gently. Cover and chill in the refrigerator for at least 3 hours. Ⓐ
4. Make the cranachan: whip the two creams together until they form soft peaks, add the vanilla, then fold in the sugar and all but 2 teaspoons of the toasted oatmeal.
5. Spoon the cranachan into a dish and sprinkle with the reserved oatmeal. Serve with the chilled kissel.

Ⓐ The kissel can be prepared up to 24 hours in advance.

FROM THE TOP Winter rhubarb jelly; Cranachan with fruit kissel; Melon and raspberries in sauternes

BRANDY JUNKET WITH GREEN FRUIT SALAD

Brandy junket:	75g (3oz) green grapes, halved and seeded
450ml (¾ pint) milk	
150ml (5fl oz) single cream	2 Kiwi fruit, peeled and sliced
1 tablespoon light soft brown sugar	2 Feijoa fruit, peeled and sliced (or lychees, peeled and stoned)
2 tablespoons brandy	
1 teaspoon vegetarian junket rennet	½ Galia melon, peeled and cut into 1 cm (½ inch) cubes
freshly grated nutmeg	2 crisp green apples, unpeeled, quartered, cored and sliced
Green fruit salad:	
50g (2oz) caster sugar	
150ml (5fl oz) water	sprigs of fresh mint, to decorate
1 tablespoon lemon juice	

Preparation time: *30 minutes, plus standing and chilling*
Cooking time: *5 minutes*

This junket, a sophisticated version of the gentle childhood pudding, should be set in small dishes, and the fruit salad should be served in one large dish, so that the two are served separately but enjoyed together. The junket may be made without brandy if preferred. Feijoa fruit can be found in some greengrocers and large supermarkets.
1. Make the junket. Pour the milk and cream into a pan and warm until just tepid (36°C/98°F). Stir in the sugar until dissolved then add the brandy and rennet essence.
2. Pour the junket into 4 small dishes, grate a little nutmeg on top of each one and leave to stand at room temperature for about 1 hour to set, then chill in the refrigerator for at least 3 hours. Ⓐ
3. Make the fruit salad. Put the sugar, water and lemon juice into a small pan, bring to the boil and simmer for 1 minute. Leave until cold.
4. Arrange the fruits in a dish and pour the cold syrup over. Cover and refrigerate until ready to serve with the junkets. Ⓐ
5. Decorate the fruit salad with mint before serving.
Ⓐ Both the junket and fruit salad can be prepared up to 8 hours in advance, covered and kept in the refrigerator.

STRAWBERRY AND YOGURT ICE

100g (4oz) caster sugar	1 egg white
300ml (½ pint) water	150ml (5fl oz) double or whipping cream
350g (12oz) fresh strawberries	
300ml (½ pint) strawberry yogurt	

Preparation time: *25 minutes, plus freezing*
Cooking time: *10 minutes*

BOILING SUGAR SYRUP FOR ICE CREAM

When boiling sugar syrup the thread stage temperature is 107°C/225°F, on a sugar boiling thermometer. To test without a thermometer remove a little of the syrup with a small spoon and allow it to fall from the spoon on to a dish. The syrup should form a fine thread.

A light ice cream, not too rich and with a strong fruity taste. The egg white makes it go a little further and lightens the texture.
1. Put the sugar and water into a small pan and heat gently to dissolve the sugar, then boil rapidly until the thread stage is reached (see hint box). Leave to cool.
2. Reserve 4 strawberries for decoration, slice the rest and put into a blender or food processor with the syrup. Blend for a few seconds and pour into a bowl.
3. Stir the yogurt into the strawberries and pour into a 1.2 litre (2 pint) freezer container. Freeze for about 2 hours, stirring once or twice, until mushy.
4. Spoon the strawberry mixture into a large mixing bowl and put the egg white and cream into slightly smaller bowls.
5. Using an electric whisk, beat the egg white until stiff but not dry. Whisk the cream until it forms soft peaks, and beat the strawberry mixture until smooth. There is no need to wash the whisk in between if you keep to this order.
6. With a large metal spoon turn the egg white and cream into the strawberry mixture and gently fold all three together until smoothly blended.
7. Pour into the container and freeze for about 3 hours until the ice cream is setting round the edges. Spoon into a bowl and whisk again until smooth and light (this prevents crystals forming in the ice cream).
8. Pour back into the container, cover and freeze for at least 6 hours. Ⓕ
9. Take the ice cream from the freezer about 40 minutes before serving and transfer to the refrigerator to soften slightly. Scoop or spoon the ice cream into glasses and serve decorated with the reserved strawberries.
Ⓕ Can be frozen for 1 month.

CLOCKWISE FROM RIGHT Cider pears with passion fruit; Strawberry and yogurt ice; Brandy junket with green fruit salad

CIDER PEARS WITH PASSION FRUIT

4 large ripe pears	2 tablespoons clear honey
pared strips of rind from 1 lemon	4 ripe passion fruit
300 ml (½ pint) dry cider	

Preparation time: *10 minutes, plus chilling*
Cooking time: *15 minutes*

A simple recipe using fresh pears with the tropical taste of passion fruit. Quite delicious.

1. Peel and halve the pears. Cut a long V shape to remove the woody stalk and scoop out the core with a teaspoon.
2. Put the pear halves in a large pan, cut side up. Add the strips of lemon rind then pour the cider and honey over.
3. Bring slowly to the boil, cover the pan and lower the heat. Simmer gently for about 10 minutes until the pears are tender.
4. Lift the pears from the syrup with a slotted spoon and arrange them in a shallow serving dish.
5. Remove the lemon rind from the syrup, turn the heat up and boil quickly for 5 minutes to reduce it a little. Leave it to cool for a few minutes.
6. Cut the passion fruit in half, scoop the seeds and flesh into the syrup, stir briefly, then spoon over the pears. Cover, and chill in the refrigerator for about 3 hours before serving. Ⓐ
Ⓐ Can be left to chill for up to 24 hours.

PEARS BRÛLÉE

4 ripe pears	150 ml (5 fl oz) natural yogurt
300 ml (½ pint) red wine	100 g (4 oz) light soft brown sugar
75 g (3 oz) light soft brown sugar	
2 teaspoons arrowroot or cornflour	
2 tablespoons water	
300 ml (½ pint) double or whipping cream	

Preparation time: *20 minutes, plus cooling and chilling*
Cooking time: *15 minutes*

This delicious combination of two classic recipes is perfect for a dinner party. It is best served in individual portions but can also be made in one large shallow ovenproof dish.
1. Quarter, peel and core the pears and halve each quarter.
2. Place in a large pan with the wine and sugar and bring slowly to the boil, making sure that the sugar has dissolved. Simmer, covered, for about 10 minutes until the pears are just tender.
3. Remove the pears with a slotted spoon and arrange in 4 small ovenproof dishes.
4. Turn up the heat and boil the wine syrup quickly to reduce to about 150 ml (5 fl oz). Blend the arrowroot with the water and stir into the syrup. Boil for 1 minute until the syrup clears and thickens.
5. Spoon some syrup over each dish and leave in the refrigerator for 1 hour.
6. Whip the cream until it forms soft peaks, but take care not to overwhip. Beat the yogurt until smooth then fold into the cream.
7. Spoon the cream and yogurt on to the 4 dishes, covering the pears completely. Cover and chill in the refrigerator for a minimum of 4 hours.
8. Sprinkle the sugar evenly all over the cream and place the dishes under a preheated grill for about 2 minutes until the sugar is caramelized.
9. Cool and chill again for 2 hours before serving.

ORANGES IN APRICOT LIQUEUR

Using a serrated knife, cut the top and bottom off 4 oranges, place each one flat on a plate and cut away the skin and pith. Cut into segments by cutting down on either side of each membrane and place the segments in a bowl with any juice from the plate. Stir in 4-6 tablespoons of apricot liqueur (or use orange liqueur if more convenient), cover and chill in the refrigerator for 3-4 hours.

APRICOT AND ORANGE SORBET

Serves 6-8	1 egg white
150 g (5 oz) caster sugar	orange slices, to decorate (optional)
300 ml (½ pint) water	
85 ml (3 fl oz) orange juice	
3 tablespoons lemon juice	
grated rind of 1 orange	
500 g (1¼ lb) ripe apricots, halved and stoned	

Preparation time: *20 minutes, plus cooling and freezing*
Cooking time: *8 minutes*

Serve this fruity ice on its own, or with fresh oranges that have been steeped in apricot liqueur (see hint box).
1. Put the sugar, water, orange and lemon juices and orange rind into a pan and bring to the boil, stirring until the sugar has dissolved.
2. Increase the heat and boil rapidly for about 5 minutes until the thread stage is reached (see page 68).

3. Add the apricots and simmer gently for 2 minutes until they have softened slightly. Leave them to cool in the syrup.

4. Pour the fruit and syrup into a liquidizer or food processor and blend until smooth.

5. Pour into a freezer container, cover and freeze for about 2 hours until frozen round the sides but mushy in the centre.

6. Tip into a basin and whisk briefly until smooth. Whisk the egg white until it forms soft peaks and fold into the fruit using a metal spoon.

7. Pour back into the container and freeze for about 6 hours. F

8. About 1 hour before serving take the sorbet from the freezer and put in the refrigerator to soften slightly.

9. Arrange scoops of sorbet in individual glasses and decorate with orange slices.

F Can be frozen for 1 month.

FROM THE LEFT Pears brûlée; Apricot and orange sorbet; Blackberry and almond flan

BLACKBERRY AND ALMOND FLAN

Pastry:

75 g (3 oz) plain wholemeal flour

75 g (3 oz) plain white flour

pinch of salt

75 g (3 oz) hard vegetable margarine

3 tablespoons water

1 tablespoon vegetable oil

Filling:

175 g (6 oz) fresh or thawed, frozen blackberries

25 g (1 oz) light soft brown sugar

2 teaspoons lemon juice

2 teaspoons arrowroot or cornflour

2 tablespoons water

Topping:

50 g (2 oz) soft vegetable margarine

50 g (2 oz) light soft brown sugar

1 egg, beaten

65 g (2½ oz) fresh wholewheat breadcrumbs

25 g (1 oz) ground almonds

a few drops almond essence

Decoration:

25 g (1 oz) flaked almonds

1 tablespoon caster sugar

Preparation time: *35 minutes, plus cooling*
Cooking time: *45 minutes*
Oven: *200°C, 400°F, Gas Mark 6*
Then: *180°C, 350°F, Gas Mark 4*

This flan has a delicious, wholesome autumnal flavour, reminiscent of wheatfields and hedgerows. Serve it warm with ice cream, or cold on an autumn picnic.

1. Make the pastry. Put the flours and salt into a bowl and rub in the margarine until the mixture resembles fine breadcrumbs.

2. Using a round-bladed knife, mix to a firm dough with the water and oil. The oil helps to keep wholemeal pastry moist and light.

3. Roll out the pastry on a lightly floured surface and line a 20 cm (8 inch) fluted flan ring.

4. Place the flan tin on a baking sheet and bake for 15 minutes to 'set' the pastry without browning. Remove from the oven and reduce the oven temperature.

5. Meanwhile prepare the filling. Put the blackberries, sugar and lemon juice into a small pan and cook for about 5 minutes until the juice runs.

6. Blend together the arrowroot and water and stir into the blackberries. Bring to the boil and stir gently until the mixture thickens and clears. Set aside to cool.

7. Prepare the topping. Cream together the margarine and sugar until fluffy. Beat in the egg then fold in the breadcrumbs, ground almonds and almond essence.

8. Spoon the fruit filling into the flan case and spread evenly. Arrange small spoonfuls of the topping over the fruit spreading it out a little, but there is no need to cover the fruit completely.

9. Sprinkle the flaked almonds on top, then bake for 25-30 minutes until firm and lightly browned.

10. Dredge with caster sugar while still hot and serve.

FROM THE LEFT Hot spiced peaches; Plum cheesecake; Fig and honey custard tart

HOT SPICED PEACHES

4 large ripe fresh peaches	15g (½oz) butter
grated rind of 1 lemon	
¼ teaspoon ground cinnamon	
2 tablespoons clear honey	

Preparation time: *5 minutes*
Cooking time: *15-20 minutes*
Oven: *180°C, 350°F, Gas Mark 4*

A delightful late summer pudding. Serve the peaches hot from the oven with cream or with Cranachan (page 66).
1. First skin the peaches. Dip them one at a time in boiling water and the skins will slide off very easily. Cut each peach in half and twist to separate the halves, then remove the stone.
2. Arrange the peach halves cut side up in an ovenproof dish. Sprinkle with the lemon rind and cinnamon then spoon the honey over.
3. Place a dot of butter in the cavity of each peach, cover the dish and bake for about 20 minutes until the peaches are tender and juicy.

PLUM CHEESECAKE

Serves 6-8

Base:

100 g (4 oz) self-raising flour

25 g (1 oz) light soft brown sugar

50 g (2 oz) hard vegetable margarine

2 tablespoons vegetable oil

Filling:

450 g (1 lb) ripe red plums, halved and stoned

¼ teaspoon ground cinnamon

225 g (8 oz) Quark or other low-fat soft cheese

100 g (4 oz) light soft brown sugar

2 teaspoons vanilla essence

150 ml (5 fl oz) soured cream

1 tablespoon plain white flour

3 eggs, separated

icing sugar, for dusting

Preparation time: *40 minutes, plus cooling and chilling (optional)*

Cooking time: *1¼ hours*

Oven: *180°C, 350°F, Gas Mark 4*

Then: *160°C, 325°F, Gas Mark 3*

Quark is a soft cheese made with skimmed milk and thus is very low in fat. It is now available in health food shops and most large supermarkets, but the cheesecake is equally good made with curd cheese if you prefer it. The cheesecake will rise in the oven and drop slowly as it cools, cracking slightly. Do not worry, this is just as it should be.

1. First prepare the base. Put the flour, sugar, margarine and oil into a bowl and knead it all together to form a soft dough. Press the dough evenly over the base of a greased loose-bottomed 20 cm (8 inch) cake tin.

2. Bake near the top of the oven for 20 minutes until golden brown. Remove and leave to cool in the tin. Reduce the oven temperature.

3. Arrange the plum halves close together over the base in the tin, cut-side down. Sprinkle with the cinnamon.

4. While the base is cooking make the filling. Put the quark or curd cheese, 50 g (2 oz) of the sugar, vanilla essence, soured cream, flour and egg yolks into a bowl and whisk together until blended.

5. In another bowl whisk the egg whites until stiff then whisk in the remaining 50 g (2 oz) sugar. Fold lightly into the cheese mixture and spoon into the tin, over the plums.

6. Bake in the centre of the oven for 1¼ hours until the top is brown and firm to the touch then turn off the oven and slightly open the door. Leave the cheesecake to cool in the open oven for 1 hour.

7. Run a knife round the edge of the cheesecake to loosen it and gently ease it out of the tin.

8. Slide the cheesecake on to a serving plate and chill in the refrigerator for up to 3 hours before serving, if time allows. [A]

9. Dust very lightly with icing sugar before serving.

[A] Can be left to chill in the refrigerator for up to 24 hours, but take from the refrigerator an hour before serving.

FIG AND HONEY CUSTARD TART

Pastry:

75 g (3 oz) plain wholewheat flour

75 g (3 oz) plain white flour

pinch of salt

75 g (3 oz) hard vegetable margarine

1 egg yolk

1 tablespoon water

1 tablespoon vegetable oil

Filling:

175 g (6 oz) dried figs

3 tablespoons clear honey

1 tablespoon lemon juice

150 ml (5 fl oz) single cream

4 tablespoons milk

1 egg, beaten

1 tablespoon coarsely chopped walnuts

Preparation time: *20 minutes, plus soaking*

Cooking time: *35 minutes*

Oven: *200°C, 400°F, Gas Mark 6*

Then: *190°C, 375°F, Gas Mark 5*

Use whole loose figs for this recipe if possible; the moist ready-to-eat variety that are sold in sealed packs.

1. Put the flours and salt into a bowl and rub in the margarine until the mixture resembles fine breadcrumbs. Make a well in the centre, add the egg yolk, water and oil. Mix to a dough, using a round-bladed knife.

2. Roll out the pastry on a floured surface and line a 20 cm (8 inch) fluted flan ring. Place on a baking tray.

3. Bake the flan case for 15 minutes to set the pastry without browning. Remove and cool in the tin on a wire tray. Reduce the oven temperature.

4. Meanwhile prepare the filling. Cut the figs into slices, removing the hard stalk top. Put them in a small bowl with the honey and lemon juice, stir well, cover and leave to soak for about an hour to absorb most of the liquid.

5. Spoon the figs into the flan and arrange evenly over the cooked pastry case.

6. Stir the cream and milk into the beaten egg. Pour over the figs and sprinkle the walnuts on the top.

7. Bake for about 20 minutes, until the custard is just set and not browned. Cool in the tin on a wire tray.

8. Serve warm or cold.

·C·A·K·E·S & B·I·S·C·U·I·T·S·

FRUITY BARS

Makes about 450g (1 lb)
175g (6 oz) best quality dried apricots, finely chopped
50g (2 oz) seedless raisins, finely chopped
50g (2 oz) pecan nuts, finely chopped
50g (2 oz) ground hazelnuts
grated rind of 1 orange
2 dessertspoons clear honey

about 2 dessertspoons lemon juice
icing sugar, for dusting

Preparation time: *15 minutes, plus chilling*

So easy to make, these fruity little petit fours are delicious with coffee. Cut into slices they would make a special treat for a packed lunch.
1. Combine the apricots, raisins, pecan nuts, hazelnuts and orange rind in a small bowl.
2. Mix in all the honey and 1 dessertspoon of the lemon juice. Stir in the remaining juice gradually until the mixture is a firm paste.
3. Turn the mixture on to a piece of baking foil and pat into an oblong shape about 2 cm (¾ inch) thick.
4. Wrap the foil round to make a flat packet and refrigerate for about 3 hours until firm. Ⓐ
5. Remove the foil and cut the fruit and nut bar with a sharp knife into small pieces about 1 cm (½ inch) wide and 4 cm (1½ inches) long.
6. Dust lightly with icing sugar before serving.
Ⓐ The mixture can be left to chill in the refrigerator for up to 36 hours.

LEMON AND ALMOND CAKE

Makes one 23 cm (9 inch) round cake
25g (1 oz) flaked almonds
100g (4 oz) soft vegetable margarine
100g (4 oz) light soft brown sugar
2 eggs, beaten
grated rind of 1 lemon
100g (4 oz) wholemeal self-raising flour

Syrup:
75g (3 oz) caster sugar
3-4 tablespoons fresh lemon juice

Preparation time: *20 minutes*
Cooking time: *20-25 minutes*
Oven: *180°C, 350°F, Gas Mark 4*

The sharp lemon syrup spooned over the hot upside-down cake gives a distinctive flavour. The cake keeps very well for a week.
1. Line the base of a round 23 cm (9 inch) sandwich tin with non-stick silicone paper or greased greaseproof paper. Thoroughly grease the sides of the tin. Tip the almonds into the tin and shake them around so that they cling to the sides and base.
2. Put the margarine and sugar into a bowl and cream them together until light and fluffy. Gradually beat in the eggs a tablespoon at a time, then beat in the lemon rind.
3. Fold in the flour until smoothly blended then spoon the mixture into the prepared tin. Smooth the top.
4. Bake near the centre of the preheated oven for 20-25 minutes until risen and firm to the touch.
5. Meanwhile prepare the syrup. Put the caster sugar into a small basin and stir in the lemon juice. Leave to stand, stirring occasionally.
6. When the cake is cooked remove from the oven and leave in the tin for 1 minute, then turn out upside down on to a wire tray and carefully peel off the lining paper.
7. Spoon the lemon syrup evenly over the hot cake, covering the nuts, allowing it to soak in.

FROM THE RIGHT Lemon and almond cake; Fruity bars

MOIST CARROT AND WALNUT CAKE

Makes one 18 cm (7 inch) round cake
225 g (8 oz) light soft brown sugar
175 ml (6 fl oz) vegetable oil
2 eggs
100 g (4 oz) plain wholemeal flour
1 teaspoon ground cinnamon
1 teaspoon bicarbonate of soda
150 g (5 oz) coarsely grated carrots
50 g (2 oz) chopped walnuts

Topping:
2 tablespoons apricot jam
1 tablespoon lemon juice
50 g (2 oz) chopped walnuts

Preparation time: *25 minutes, plus cooling*
Cooking time: *1 hour 10 minutes*
Oven: *180°C, 350°F, Gas Mark 4*

An exceptionally soft, moist cake which will keep well for up to a week. Quick to make and good even without a topping if time is short.

1. Line an 18 cm (7 inch) round cake tin with non-stick silicone paper or greased greaseproof paper. Use a fixed-base tin as the mixture is almost a pouring consistency.
2. Put the sugar into a mixing bowl and using an electric whisk gradually whisk the oil, then whisk in the eggs one at a time.
3. Mix together the flour, cinnamon and bicarbonate of soda and stir into the egg mixture, then add the carrots and walnuts.
4. Beat all the ingredients together with a wooden spoon then pour the mixture into the prepared tin.
5. Place in the centre of a preheated oven and bake for about 1 hour 10 minutes until the cake is risen and firm to the touch. Remove from the oven, leave to stand in the tin for 3 minutes, then turn out on to a wire tray, peel off the paper and leave to cool.
6. To make the topping, boil the jam and lemon juice together in a small pan for 2-3 minutes. Brush the mixture generously over the top of the cooled cake and immediately sprinkle the walnuts over. The glaze will set very quickly.
Variation:
For a traditional finish to the cake, spread the top with 50 g (2 oz) cream cheese beaten with icing sugar to taste.

LITTLE MARZIPAN AND APPLE PIES

Makes 20 pies
Pastry:
350 g (12 oz) wholemeal self-raising flour
pinch of salt
225 g (8 oz) hard vegetable margarine, from the freezer
scant 7 tablespoons water
2 tablespoons vegetable oil
Filling:
275 g (10 oz) Bramley apples, peeled, cored and coarsely chopped

100 g (4 oz) bought marzipan, cut into 5 mm (¼ inch) cubes
milk, for brushing
1 tablespoon demerara sugar (optional)

Preparation time: *35 minutes, plus chilling*
Cooking time: *20 minutes*
Oven: *220°C, 425°F, Gas mark 7*

These tempting little pies make the perfect vegetarian alternative to traditional mince pies and are best served warm.

1. Make the pastry. Put the flours and salt into a bowl. Grate the margarine straight into the flour, dipping it into the bowl now and again to free the flakes of margarine.
2. Distribute the margarine gently through the flour, using a round-bladed knife, then add the water and oil. Mix to a fairly firm dough then put into a polythene bag and chill in the refrigerator for 1 hour if possible. Ⓐ
3. Make the filling. Mix the apple and marzipan together in a bowl.
4. Roll out the pastry quite thinly on a lightly floured surface. Cut out 40 rounds using a 7½ cm (3 inch) fluted cutter.
5. Line 20 small tartlet tins with half the rounds, and spoon the filling into them, packing it well in.
6. Brush both sides of the remaining rounds with milk and lay them on top of the tartlets in the tin. Press the edges together to seal and sprinkle each one with a little demerara sugar, if liked.
7. Bake near the top of the oven for 15-20 minutes until golden brown.
8. Lift carefully from the tin and leave to cool slightly on a wire tray. Ⓕ
9. Serve warm or cold.
Ⓐ The pastry can be prepared up to 24 hours in advance but remove from the refrigerator 30 minutes before rolling out.
Ⓕ When the pies are quite cold they can be frozen for up to 1 month. They are best if thawed and warmed gently in the oven before serving.

FROM THE TOP Moist carrot and walnut cake; Little marzipan and apple pies

MIXED FRUIT LOAF

Makes one 450g (1lb) loaf	¼ teaspoon ground
75g (3oz) sultanas	cinnamon
50g (2oz) raisins	pinch of nutmeg
50g (2oz) currants	50ml (2fl oz) unsweetened
25g (1oz) dried apricots, finely chopped	orange juice
	1 egg, beaten
75g (3oz) light soft brown sugar	2 tablespoons vegetable oil
	175g (6oz) wholemeal, self-raising flour
grated rind of 1 lemon	

Preparation time: *10 minutes, plus soaking*
Cooking time: *50-60 minutes*
Oven: *160°C, 325°F, Gas Mark 3*

This quickly made loaf is a cross between bread and cake, crusty outside and moist inside. It is equally delicious plain, or spread with unsalted butter. The loaf keeps well in an airtight tin for up to 1 week.

1. Line a 450g (1lb) loaf tin with non-stick silicone or greased greaseproof paper.
2. Put the sultanas, raisins, currants and apricots into a mixing bowl and add the sugar, lemon rind, cinnamon and nutmeg.
3. Pour over the orange juice and stir well. Cover and leave the fruits to soak in the juice for about 2 hours.
4. Beat in the egg and the oil then stir in the flour. Spoon the mixture into the prepared tin and bake in the centre of the oven for 50-60 minutes.
5. Turn out on to a wire tray, peel off the paper and leave to cool completely before slicing.

SCONE RING WITH SOFT CHEESE AND FRUIT

Makes 8 scones	120ml (4fl oz) milk
100g (4oz) wholemeal self-raising flour	1 tablespoon vegetable oil
	milk, for brushing
100g (4oz) white self-raising flour	To serve:
pinch of salt	100g-175g (4-6oz) curd or cream cheese
25g (1oz) light soft brown sugar	seasonal fruits (raspberries, blackberries, strawberries or peaches)
50g (2oz) hard vegetable margarine	

Preparation time: *20 minutes, plus resting*
Cooking time: *15-20 minutes*
Oven: *220°C, 425°F, Gas Mark 7*

The addition of a little oil to the scone mix will keep the scones soft, and leaving them to rest in a warm place before baking will make them exceptionally light.

1. Mix the flours, salt and sugar in a bowl.

2. Rub in the margarine until the mixture resembles fine breadcrumbs.
3. Make a well in the centre of the mixture and pour in all the milk and oil, mixing lightly with a knife to produce a soft consistency.
4. Turn the dough on to a lightly floured surface and roll it out gently to about 2cm (¾ inch) thick. Cut out 8 scones using a 6cm (2½ inch) round fluted cutter.
5. Arrange the scones in a circle, just touching, on a floured baking tray.
6. Brush with milk and leave in a warm place for 15 minutes.
7. Bake near the top of the oven for 15 minutes until well risen and brown. Slide on to a wire tray to cool, re-shaping the circle if the scones separate.
8. To serve, place the curd or cream cheese in a small dish in the centre of the scone ring and serve with a bowl containing the fresh seasonal fruits.

FROM THE LEFT Mixed fruit loaf; Scone ring with soft cheese and fruit; Caraway and coriander biscuits

CARAWAY AND CORIANDER BISCUITS

Makes about 20
200 g (7 oz) wholemeal self-raising flour

50 g (2 oz) coarse oatmeal

50 g (2 oz) light soft brown sugar

2 teaspoons ground coriander

1 teaspoon caraway seeds

175 g (6 oz) butter, at room temperature

Preparation time: *15 minutes*
Cooking time: *20 minutes*
Oven: *160°C, 325°F, Gas Mark 3*

These crisp little oat biscuits have a distinctive flavour and are quick to make. Nice with morning coffee.

1. Put the flour, oatmeal, sugar, coriander and caraway seeds into a bowl. Cut the butter into small pieces and add to the bowl.
2. Using your hands, knead the mixture into a firm dough.
3. Roll out on a lightly floured surface to about 5 mm (¼ inch) thick. Cut out rounds using a 5 cm (2 inch) plain biscuit cutter. Gather up the trimmings, roll out again and cut out more rounds.
4. Arrange on a lightly greased baking sheet and bake near the top of the oven for about 20 minutes, until very pale brown.
5. Cool on a wire tray.

◆ I·N·D·E·X ◆

THE
VEGETARIAN
FEAST